THEATRE S
A PUBLICATION OF THE SOUTH

MW00563501

Theatre, War, and Propaganda:

1930–2005

Volume 14

Published by the

Southeastern Theatre Conference and

The University of Alabama Press

THEATRE SYMPOSIUM is published annually by the Southeastern Theatre Conference, Inc. (SETC), and The University of Alabama Press. SETC nonstudent members receive the journal as a part of their membership under rules determined by SETC. For information on membership write to SETC, P.O. Box 9868, Greensboro, NC 27429-0868. All other inquiries regarding subscriptions, circulation, purchase of individual copies, and requests to reprint materials should be addressed to The University of Alabama Press, Box 870380, Tuscaloosa, AL 35487-0380.

THEATRE SYMPOSIUM publishes works of scholarship resulting from a single-topic meeting held on a southeastern university campus each spring. A call for papers to be presented at that meeting is widely publicized each autumn for the following spring. Authors are encouraged to send unsolicited manuscripts directly to the editor. Information about the next symposium is available from the editor, Jay Malarcher, Division of Theatre and Dance, College of Creative Arts, West Virginia University, P.O. Box 6111, Morgantown, West Virginia 26506-6111; (304) 293-4841, X3126. Email: Jay.Malarcher@mail.wvu.edu.

THEATRE SYMPOSIUM
A PUBLICATION OF THE SOUTHEASTERN THEATRE CONFERENCE

Volume 14   *Contents*   **2006**

Introduction

As I write this introduction, the United States finds itself mired in the aftermath of its invasion of Iraq, its forces and representatives bombarded daily by suicide bombers and insurgents, its body politic divided between prowar *pax americana* idealists and those who view the intervention as a foolishly conceived adventurist exercise on the part of an out-of-control American imperium. The Iraq campaign follows hard on the war in Afghanistan, itself a response to a global holy war declared on the West by jihadists intent on forcing a cataclysmic confrontation between liberal humanist values and recidivist theocratic certitude. Not an auspicious beginning for the twenty-first century, but then again, what else is new? Our best efforts notwithstanding, humankind has manifestly failed to make war obsolete, despite the Pollyannaish promise of Wilson's League of Nations, the United Nations Charter, or, for that matter, the women of Athens in the fifth century BCE.

In April 2005 the SETC Theatre Symposium convened in Auburn, Alabama, to examine the relationship between theatre, war, and propaganda. Given the current state of world politics, I was not surprised that the topic sparked such an enthusiastic response, with scholars coming from as far away as Paris, Vienna, and Cairo. But I suspect that even in a time of relative peace the subject would resonate. Theatre, as we who teach introductory courses tell our students repeatedly, is conflict, and the most extreme example of human conflict is, inarguably, war. For twenty-five hundred years, from Aristophanes' *Lysistrata* to Shakespeare's *Henry V* to the street theatre and protest drama of the Vietnam era, war has provided compelling fodder—"canon" fodder, if you will—

for playwrights and performers. War itself is conducted in various "theatres" and in recent years has become fully televised, the ultimate "reality" program, a spectator sport for armchair combatants. So, too, can theatre be an ideal form of propaganda, a mouthpiece for antiwar resistance or, to paraphrase Clausewitz, a continuation of armed conflict by other means.

As always, this year's symposium covered a rich and diverse mix of subtopics, many of which, because of space limitations and publication conflicts, cannot be represented in this volume. I am unable, for example, to share Frank Bradley's discussion of the complex censorship issues involved in American University in Cairo's controversial production of *The Vagina Monologues,* James Thompson's employment of theatre performance as an instrument of peace and justice in war-ravaged Sri-Lanka, or Rebecca Rugg's compelling study of the racially charged, gender-bending World War II Irving Berlin revue *This Is the Army.* Missing also is Lisa Channer's personal narrative of her experience in directing *The Trojan Women* on a conservative southern college campus during the initial buildup to the war in Iraq, and Elizabeth Rietz Mullenix's comparison and contrast of theatrical prewar propaganda in New York and Charleston during the months between Lincoln's election and the shots fired at Fort Sumter in 1861.

The ten outstanding essays that are represented here reflect scholarly concerns that are largely American and largely twentieth-century, a tripartite examination of theatrical response to the Second World War, Vietnam, and the aftermath of 9/11. The collection begins with two articles by keynote presenters Bruce A. McConachie of the University of Pittsburgh and Alan Woods, director of Ohio State University's Jerome Lawrence and Robert E. Lee Theatre Research Institute. Appropriately, both Professor McConachie and Professor Woods examine the nature and reception of theatrical propaganda. In "A Cognitive Approach to Brechtian Theatre" McConachie takes a fresh look at the *Verfremdungseffekt,* deconstructing standard notions concerning Brecht's position on spectator empathy and positing the concept of "meta-response" as a basis for understanding Brechtian dialectics. In "*Porgy and Bess* as Propaganda: Preaching to the [Eva Jessye] Choir," Woods examines the postwar European tour of Robert Breen's production of *Porgy and Bess* as an example of American cold war diplomacy, an effort in which the showcasing of the production's African American cast took on a greater significance than the production itself.

The three essays that follow also cohere around the Second World War, each taking a strikingly different approach. The theatre is uniquely equipped to define and perpetuate the national mythology indispensable to a nation at war. Claudia Wilsch Case looks at the ways in which the American Theatre Guild's production of *Oklahoma!* defined a morale-boosting conception of the American "heartland" during the darkest days of the conflict. Anne Fletcher's delightful reading of Thornton Wilder's *Our Town* and William Saroyan's *The Time of Your Life* invite us to reexamine these prewar texts and productions in light of Buddhism and phenomenology. Fletcher juxtaposes what she sees as "the contemplative, the compassionate, the comic, and the sublime" nature of these plays with the turbulent political climate engendered by the impending world conflagration. Kb Saine documents the somewhat bizarre efforts of the U.S. military to build and foster morale in newly integrated camps through the production of fully subsidized minstrel shows.

Kate Bredeson, Jim Stacy, and David Callaghan tackle the subject of Vietnam-era protest drama. Bredeson documents the explosive reaction in Avignon during the summer of 1968, when authorities banned the Chêne Noir company's production of Gérard Gelas's *La paillasse aux seins nus* and, later, the Living Theatre's production of *Paradise Now.* The street protests that followed the bans turned the city of Avignon itself into a theatrical spectacle and mirrored the unrest that had erupted on the streets of Paris earlier that year. Stacy's concerns are with the theatrical "iterations" that followed from the symbolic burning of Maryland draft records by Daniel and Philip Berrigan and the Catonsville Nine, also in 1968, whereas Callaghan grapples with the contrast between the vibrant and energetic reaction to the war in Vietnam by American avant-garde theatre artists and the restrained—some might say tepid—theatrical response to the war in Iraq.

Callaghan's task is problematic, if only because of the lack of historical distance afforded by the current conflict. Similarly, the first flurry of plays produced in the aftermath of the 9/11 attacks addressed the significance of a tragedy so fresh as to preclude anything other than a visceral response. Evan Bridenstine argues that the immediacy of the "first wave" of plays that followed in the wake of 9/11 has given way to a more distanced "second wave," and he examines the ways in which these more recent plays have problematized the difficulties that arise when national trauma forces a conflict between the subject's status as an individual and his or her position as a member of a national or cultural group. Finally, Diana Calderazzo reminds us of the importance of context in the production of meaning, particularly in times of national crisis. Calderazzo explores the critical reactions to Stephen Sondheim's *Assassins,* both in the United States and abroad, and how those reactions were informed by events such as the 1991 Gulf War, the 9/11 attacks, and, in the case of the 1998 Israeli production, the assassination of Prime Minister Yitzhak Rabin.

As the editor of this volume I am indebted to a number of people who have helped me in ways both tangible and intangible throughout the process. I would particularly like to thank Auburn University and Tony Carey of the College of Liberal Arts for support of the symposium event; I also thank Worth Gardner and the faculty of the Auburn University Department of Theatre for their forbearance and support in allowing me the time to do this job, Linda Bell for her help with the cover photograph, and all of the members, past and present, of the Symposium Steering Committee who offered advice and consultation throughout. I am especially grateful to Susan Kattwinkel and Phil Hill, both former editors of *Theatre Symposium,* for all of their guidance and advice. Finally, I would like to publicly thank SETC executive director Betsey Baun, past president Tony Haigh, and current president Denise Halbach for the advocacy and support that have made this volume possible.

M. SCOTT PHILLIPS
AUBURN UNIVERSITY

A Cognitive Approach

to Brechtian Theatre

Bruce A. McConachie

A s THIS CONFERENCE DEMONSTRATES, antiwar plays come in all shapes and sizes. Among the kinds of antiwar plays that most theatre historians and critics view as different animals, perhaps few are thought to be as far apart as realist and Brechtian theatre. It is a general truism in our tribe of scholars that realism creates passive spectators, while Brecht and his allies induced active spectating. According to Brecht, realist theatre, based on Aristotelian principles, relies primarily on empathy and identification to naturalize the historical world and consequently inhibits the desire to change it. In contrast, Brecht held that his epic theatre could distance the spectator from historical realities and make them appear strange rather than natural. Once *Verfremdung* takes *Effekt,* the spectator gains agency and perhaps the possibility to help make genuine historical change. If you are like me, you have repeated this truism to your students for years, using a blackboard (or a PowerPoint presentation) to contrast the characteristics of what Brecht called "epic" to his notion of "Aristotelian" theatre.

Today I want to complicate and even partly erase (or delete) this Brechtian chart that floats in all of our heads. I hope to replace some of it with insights from another field, the field of cognitive science. Brecht's notion of epic theatre relied on an understanding of theatrical reception that conflicts with significant findings in neuroscience and cognitive psychology concerning make-believe situations, empathy, and emotion. Nevertheless, despite Brecht's misunderstandings about audience response, the cognitive and historical evidence suggests that his theatre still worked to change minds and motivate political action. How it did this for spectators, however, was probably very different from what

Brecht supposed. Surprisingly, in fact, Brecht's drama induced responses that have much in common with a certain kind of realist theatre.

In what follows I will refer to significant cognitive findings relevant to spectatorship and apply them to specific scenes in Brecht's productions of *Mother Courage and Her Children*. For this I will primarily rely on the Ralph Manheim translation of the script and Brecht's 1956 model book, which he based on the original production of *Mother Courage* in 1949 and subsequent stagings by the Berliner Ensemble.[1] Where appropriate, I will also comment on Brecht's theoretical musings concerning *Verfremdungseffekt* and its relation to this spectatorial response. Finally, I will deploy some of the same cognitive insights to probe the probable response of audiences to David Rabe's *Streamers* (1975), another antiwar play but one that all critics would agree is forthrightly realist in its style and strategies. Both plays, despite very different theatrical modes, depend fundamentally on empathy, emotion, and especially metaresponse to win the hearts and minds of their audiences.

For an initial overview of the general dynamics of spectatorship, I will draw on the work of Gilles Fauconnier and Mark Turner, a cognitive psychologist and a literary scholar, whose coauthored book *The Way We Think: Conceptual Blending and the Mind's Hidden Complexities* is one of the few in cognitive studies to tackle directly the problem of theatrical doubleness. By *doubleness* I mean simply the ability of audiences to understand that performers exist simultaneously in both real and fictitious time-space; actors are real people on a stage in the present, and they are also the roles they represent in a make-believe space and time. Turner and Fauconnier demonstrate that actors can engage in theatrical doubleness and that spectators can understand it because of the ability of human beings to do "conceptual blending," the mental synthesizing of concepts from different areas of cognition. This process, ubiquitous in human imagination, occurs nearly automatically and mostly below the level of consciousness. This means that audience members do not "willingly suspend their disbelief" when they enjoy the actor's doubleness; conscious "willing" begins the process of spectating, but after spectators have accepted the frame of performance, "willing" has very little to do with it. Indeed, consciousness would only slow down cognitive processing.[2]

Instead, actors and spectators unconsciously create a third space, distinct from the perception of themselves in real time-space and the knowledge that they are playing a game of make-believe. In this third space information from both of those prior domains can be "blended" together to create perceptions that are distinct from the other two. In experiencing a dramatic performance, spectators and actors mostly "live in the blend," according to Turner and Fauconnier:

> The spectator will live in the blend only by selective projection: Many aspects of her existence (such as sitting in a seat, next to other people, in the dark), although independently available to her, are not to be projected to the blend. . . . The actor, meanwhile, is engaged in a different kind of blend, one in which his motor patterns and power of speech come directly into play, but not his free will or his foreknowledge of the [dramatic] outcome. In the blend, he says just what the character says and is surprised night after night by the same events.[3]

The mind's/brain's ability to project and compress information into a blend that constitutes a person's mental image of a millisecond of a performance defies most notions of mimesis that our field currently entertains. Cognitive blending is perhaps closest to the ideas of Kendall Walton, an aesthetic philosopher who has written extensively on the ways in which spectators participate in "authorized games of make-believe."[4]

What the human mind blends together, it can also pull apart. The spectator above hears something amusing onstage, slips out of the blend to perceive others laughing, and begins to laugh herself. The actor hears the laughter, momentarily suspends his own blend to accommodate it, and then plunges back into the behavior of the character. Actors and spectators drop in and out of their blends throughout every performance, interacting to sustain and/or modify their enjoyment of theatrical doubleness. According to Turner and Fauconnier cognitive blending structures and enables all games of make-believe, from playing with dolls to professional football. As far as cognitive scientists can tell, blending is a uniquely human ability; the minds/brains of other animals do not allow for it.

Deriving theatrical doubleness from cognitive blending may seem innocuous and even commonsensical, but it hides bombshells for several performance theories, Brechtian theatre among them. The link between theatricality and blending complicates the usual distinctions dividing realist from overtly theatrical productions and so-called passive from active spectators. Given cognitive blending, it is clear that all plays onstage involve spectator recognition of theatrical framing. As Erving Goffman understood, such frames implicitly separate everyday realities from realities that are meant to be understood as distinctive kinds of practices and events.[5] In the theatre some productions may invite spectators to move in and out of various blended frames more than others, but this is a difference in degree, not in kind. Consequently, it is unlikely that formal differences in the degree of theatricality—that is, the number and kinds of blended frames—have much to do with the political efficacy of certain kinds of theatre.

The spectator's ability to blend inputs from various cognitive realities potentially neutralizes the political activation that Brecht expected from his Verfremdungseffekt in the theatre. For *Mother Courage,* as with many of his productions, Brecht enclosed the fictitious drama of his play within the constructed artistry of the theatre. His preferred setting for the play, as noted in his model book, emphasized the theatrical work of the carpenters, technicians, designers, and others at the Berliner Ensemble. As in the original production in Zurich during the war, designed by Teo Otto, Brecht deployed screens made of seventeenth-century military equipment lashed together and placed on each side of the proscenium. Necessary scenic units, such as the presbytery and the peasants' house, were built realistically, noted Brecht, but in "artistic abbreviation."[6] The main scenic piece, of course, was the wagon, which traveled during the performance on a revolving stage to indicate its movement across Europe and from scene to scene. Technicians lowered signs from the flies to indicate the place of the present action. A half curtain cut across part of the proscenium, opening between many scenes; it left some of the mechanics of the theatre open to spectatorial view.

By emphasizing the designed, constructed nature of the set, and of his theatrical conventions generally, Brecht wanted to undermine realist illusion and keep the spectator aware of her or his potential agency in history. This goal is evident in a crucial passage from "The Mother Courage Model":

> Too much heightening of the illusion in the setting, along with a "magnetic" manner of acting which gives the spectator the illusion of being present at a fleeting, fortuitous "real" event, create such an impression of naturalness that one can no longer interpose one's judgment, imagination or reactions, and must simply conform by sharing in the experience and becoming one of "nature's" objects. The illusion created by the theatre must be a partial one, so that it can always be recognized as illusion. Reality, however completely represented, must be changed by art, in order that it may seem to be subject to change and treated as such.[7]

Brecht's aim, finally, was to turn his audience into artists so that they might redesign society and history in much the same way that the Berliner Ensemble's artistry had crafted a production of *Mother Courage.*

As critic-historian John Rouse notes, Brecht hoped to instill in his audience a desire to "swap a contradictory world for a consistent one, one that they scarcely know of for one of which they can dream."[8]

Brecht's treatment of the musical interludes in the play followed from this intention. As the model book notes, technicians "lowered a musical emblem from the flies" to tell the audience when it was time for the musicians to play. "We made use of it as a visible sign of the shift to another artistic level," Brecht said.[9] With the music playing, Helene Weigel or another actor stepped out of the momentary illusion of playing a character to sing a song directly to the spectators, much as a cabaret singer worked directly with an audience. Brecht evidently hoped that this shifting from a modified realist scene within the fictitious world of the play to a cabaret frame for the onstage action would keep the audience more conscious of the choices made by the artists and get audience members to listen more closely to the words of the song.

It is clear from Turner and Fauconnier, however, that audiences do frame-shifting all the time while watching a play. Although Brecht sought to clarify the differences between social reality and theatrical illusion for his spectators, cognitive blending does not work within this logic. The blend of performance momentarily suspends such real-life considerations to create a third space that easily mixes input from both realms. Cognitively speaking, audiences that understand the games of theatre can accommodate the differences between the realities of flesh-and-blood actors and constructed scenery and the obviously fictitious and artistic nature of the theatrical illusion. Furthermore, cognitive blending is an unconscious activity that does not, by itself, produce a jolt of recognition about historical agency. It is likely, then, that most spectators simply blended together what Brecht hoped would remain separate and lead to their mutual estrangement. Although spectators probably enjoyed the variety in theatrical modes that such shifts involved, Brecht wanted these moments to do more than provide variation. Brechtian theatre may indeed pack a certain kind of political punch, but this is not due to the frame-shifting qualities of Verfremdungseffekt, at least not for most spectators.

(At this point, it is necessary to introduce a parenthetical statement concerning the likely differences in perception between students of Brecht and average spectators who go to the theatre ignorant of his intentions. People who know what Brecht was trying to do can see Verfremdungseffekt at work in productions of *Mother Courage* if they wish. The mind is amazingly flexible in this regard. For the same reason, people who believe in the truths of semiotics can find signs and sign systems in every production without too much trouble. In these cases our minds have tricked us into believing that Verfremdungseffekt or semiotics is the natural way of spectating. But just because we can read such conceptions into our responses to a performance, this does not mean that other people must be doing it, too. Beneath both imposed abstractions, cognitive blending provides the default mode of spectating. We can complicate this foundational mode with other theories, if we wish, but we must be careful not to suppose that others see performance through the lens of our glasses.)

Part of Brecht's interest in undercutting theatrical illusionism was to limit the empathetic involvement of his audience. In his comments on Kattrin's drum scene near the end of the play, when Courage's daughter is shot and killed after beating on a drum to save the children of Halle from slaughter, Brecht recognized that audiences would be empathetically involved in the action. He stated: "In reality the epic theatre, while capable of portraying other things than stirring incidents, clashes, conspiracies, psychological torments and so on, is also capable of portraying these. Spectators may identify themselves with Kattrin in this scene; empathy may give them the happy feeling that they too possess such strength. But they are not likely to have experienced such empathy throughout the play—in the first scenes for example."[10] In this passage from the model book Brecht conflates empathy with sympathy; not only will audiences put themselves in Kattrin's shoes, but they will also consciously take her side and hope that she gains a victory. Most scholars in cognitive studies now distinguish between these two modes of relationship with others. Sympathetic engagement generally arises out of concern for another person, involves "feeling with" the other, and triggers the desire that the other person's interests will be satisfied. Empathy may lead to sympathy, but the two are not the same.[11] Brecht's confusion about the two modes was hardly unique to him. The conflation of empathy with sympathy can be traced to Locke, Hutchinson, Smith, and other philosophers of sentiment in the eighteenth-century English Enlightenment. It continues to this day.[12]

Most cognitive psychologists and philosophers, however, now draw careful distinctions between empathy and sympathy. Recent psychological and philosophical investigations have established an emerging consensus about empathy. Although theatre scholars have long speculated about its importance for audience members, the new definition of *empathy* as a foundational, nonsymbolic means of knowing the world obviates many of its earlier entailments and the objections to them by modernists such as Brecht. Empathy still involves the general ability to put yourself "in another person's shoes" and see the world from that point of view. Now, however, it is clear that people can engage others along a continuum of empathetic responses, from fleeting and "cool" to long-term and "warm-hearted." Empathy is natural, easy, ubiquitous, and mostly unconscious; within the new understanding of empathy, people no longer require a champion who shares their values before they begin empathizing.

Robert Gordon, Antonio Damasio, and Georg Vielmetter are among the prominent scholars forging this new consensus about empathy. In Gordon's influential synthesis, which spells out the epistemological implications of empirically based psychological experiments on empathy, empathic projection is a commonplace mode of understanding others through a "personal transformation" involving a shift in the viewer's "egocentric map" that can take account of "relevant differences" between the self and another.[13] Neuroscientist Damasio discusses the "mirror neurons" in the brain that not only facilitate direct empathy with another but can also be engaged to "trick" the brain into mirroring "as-if-body states," such as those created by actors who embody their characters.[14] Following Damasio, it is clear that spectators at the theatre can also mentally simulate the actions of a performer and experience the same emotions without replicating the performer's physical state.

Desiring to elide the traditional participant-observer model for gaining knowledge in the social sciences, Georg Vielmetter builds on Gordon's insights to craft a theory in which "empathetic observation" provides a natural mode of gathering information about the behavior, emotions, and beliefs of cultural others. Initial insights gained through empathy can later be tested and refined by subsequent empathetic observations, as well as through symbolic reasoning. For Vielmetter, however, empathetic probes of the same people over time remain the best way to build and refine knowledge of others.[15]

Vielmetter's "empathetic observation" gets us close to the sequential, self-correcting cognitive processes of much theatrical spectatorship. Among its other functions the cognitive blending that sets a performance apart from other human activities invites spectators to anticipate heightened, controlled, and socially sanctioned possibilities for empathetic observation. In effect, the frame of theatre is itself a major inducement for empathic projection. Because the theatre provides a safe haven for empathy and because human beings use empathy all the time to figure out other people's desires, emotions, and expectations, spectatorial empathy will begin as soon as the performance starts. Spectators will engage in what Gordon calls "lower forms" of empathy—such as facial mimicry and following the gaze of others—simply to orient themselves to the actor-characters and their world. As Gordon notes, facial

empathy is especially important in assisting us "in interpreting, predict-
ing, and explaining behavior."[16] In most performances, spectators key
in to the faces of actor-characters throughout the play to gain tenta-
tive insight into their emotions and points of view. Then, like Vielmetter's empathetic anthropologist, audiences test and refine their insights
through subsequent observations (based on dialogue, spatial relations,
and the many other ways that theatre communicates), plus ongoing empathetic probes.

From this new perspective Brecht's concerns about empathy were misplaced. Audiences begin empathizing with actors as soon as they set
foot on the stage. Brecht's first stage direction for actors in *Mother Courage* reads, "A sergeant and a recruiter stand shivering."[17] Without knowing or consciously choosing to do so, people will generally empathize
with others who are shivering; an audience in the theatre would too.
Later in the scene, when Elif and Swiss Cheese drag on Courage's
wagon, audiences would have empathized with their muscular exertion.
Both of these activities likely induced a low-level empathic response
from spectators. It is clear that Brecht understood and even welcomed
this kind of response from audiences, but he did not call it empathy.
He enjoyed the physical exertion of sporting events and wanted his
theatre spectators to watch a play in much the same manner as he observed a good boxing match. Had the definition of empathy shifted
while Brecht was alive to include these kinds of responses, he probably
would not have discarded empathy as a legitimate response in the theatre.

Spectatorial empathy always triggers emotion. In its simplest form
spectators unconsciously catch the emotions of the actor-characters with
whom they are empathizing. Following the results of empirical psychological studies, Gordon calls this "emotional contagion"; "you can catch
an emotion just as you can catch a cold, without knowing whom you
caught it from," he says.[18] The entire range of human emotions is available through "low-level" empathy. Damasio discusses three general categories of emotion and the emotions within each category; all are legible
through muscle tension and tone of voice. The first is "background
emotion" and relates to a general level of energy. Spectators can usually
intuit such background emotions as malaise, excitement, edginess, and
tranquility in actor-characters through empathy. Like many other re-
searchers, Damasio lists six "basic emotions": fear, anger, disgust, surprise, sadness, and happiness. His third category, "social emotions," includes envy, gratitude, embarrassment, jealousy, contempt, and similar
responses. Damasio provides convincing evidence that these emotional
categories tend to be "nested" within each other; background emotions
provide a general physical mode for the expression of basic emotions,

which, in turn, may produce more specific social emotions. Thus the social emotion of contempt rests within the basic emotion of disgust, and both are related to background malaise. Consequently, when actor-characters and empathetic spectators actually experience emotions, the categories of background, basic, and social tend to merge into a continuum and may be impossible to distinguish in any formal sense.

As Damasio explains, people in all cultures experience the same emotions and probably have for many centuries; the part of the brain that produces emotional responses was one of the earliest to evolve. This is because the basic emotions are linked to human survival. The fact that we are hardwired to experience emotions directly without conscious thought probably saved thousands of our ancestors. In the 1960s Paul Ekman's cross-cultural studies of emotion demonstrated that all people share the same basic emotions and express them in the same ways, regardless of cultural differences.[19] While the circumstances that may cause background, basic, and social emotions change somewhat from culture to culture, spectators would have no difficulty intuiting and sharing them with actors-characters. In performance, then, spectators catch emotions through empathy and express them physically all the time without knowing what they have "caught."

As is already apparent, Brecht preferred cool reason to rash emotion in spectatorial response. Curiously, however, "The Mother Courage Model" for the Swiss Cheese scene underlines several instances of strong emotion onstage that spectators would certainly have caught empathetically from the actors. The first, perhaps, was surprise, when a "surprise attack" from the Catholics catches Courage, Kattrin, the Cook, and others literally by surprise and sends most characters "running and shouting" around the stage. Brecht also recognized that the audience felt sadness when Swiss Cheese is taken away by the soldiers. Because he shows no foreboding, said Brecht, "that is what makes him so moving when he is taken." When Yvette hauls in the Old Colonel who is willing to buy Courage's wagon for her so that Courage can get the money for a bribe, Brecht used this incident in the performance to comment on the disgust that the audience felt for the Colonel. The actor playing the Colonel, said Brecht, "produced a striking effect with his stick. In his passionate moments, he pressed it to the ground so hard that it bent; an instant later, it snapped straight—this suggested loathsome aggressive impotence and produced an irresistibly comic effect." Brecht noted the increasing anger of Yvette in the scene, as she haggled with the soldiers over the amount of the bribe: "Her anger changes from mere anger at Courage's attempt to swindle her by paying her out of the regimental cashbox to anger at Courage's betrayal of her son."[20]

Finally, of course, the scene climaxed in performance with Weigel's silent scream when Courage must deny that she recognizes her dead son. Brecht states in the model book: "Her look of extreme suffering after she has heard the shots, her unscreaming open mouth and backward-bent head probably derived from a press photograph of an Indian woman crouched over the body of her dead son during the shelling of Singapore."[21] Critic-theorist George Steiner's memory of this event in production remains vivid:

> As the body of her son was laid before her, she merely shook her head in mute denial. The Soldiers compelled her to look again. Again she gave no sign of recognition, only a dead stare. As the body was carried off, Weigel looked the other way and tore her mouth wide open. . . . The sound that came out was raw and terrible beyond any description I could give of it. But in fact there was no sound. . . . It was silence which screamed through the whole theatre so that the audience lowered its head as before a gust of wind.[22]

In his "Mother Courage Model" for the Swiss Cheese scene, Brecht directly alludes to four of the six primary emotions that the actors have experienced in performance—surprise, sadness, disgust, and anger—and implies that the audience will feel them, too. In addition, the scene likely evoked happiness and fear as well, although Brecht does not comment directly on them. This should not be surprising; anyone who has seen a good production of the play has been rattled by the Swiss Cheese episode. Emotions are catching.

While spectators have direct, unconscious access to all emotions through empathetic involvement, there are other modes of engagement in the theatre besides empathy that spark emotional responses. Susan Feagin's elaboration of these modes for readers of fiction in her book *Reading with Feeling* has relevance to spectatorial response in the theatre; I will adapt aspects of her discussion for my purposes. Following many scholars in cognitive studies, Feagin differentiates empathy from sympathy, but she acknowledges that low-level empathy may lead in a short time to sympathetic engagement. A spectator experiences the emotions of an actor-character, "gets to know" her or his situation and point of view, and then shifts gears to sympathize with this "person." Empathetic engagement can shift into sympathetic engagement only after spectatorial emotions rise to the level of conscious feelings, however. Following Damasio and others, Feagin distinguishes emotions from feelings on the basis of consciousness; people "feel" only when the mind forms an image of the emotions the body is experiencing.

Spectators need to reflect before extending their ability to "feel with" another.[23]

Antipathy, the opposite of sympathy, is also dependent on spectatorial feelings. Instead of hoping for the best for another person, antipathy constitutes *Schadenfreude*, enjoyment of another person's misfortune and pain. As with sympathy, the mind/brain must produce the consciousness of this enjoyment before the spectator is aware of "feeling against." Both modes of engagement can lead to the full range of emotional responses. The sympathetic mode can evoke anger, fear, disgust, and all of the other basic emotions, as well as background and social emotions. Likewise, "feeling against" an actor-character can, in the right circumstances, induce tranquility, happiness, and gratitude.

Sympathy and antipathy work primarily at the dramatic rather than the social level in most performances. That is, spectators become emotionally and feelingly involved primarily with the characters and story of the drama, not with the larger social world that contains it. Within the social mode of spectatorship, an action primarily constituted by the real world, not the fictitious one, induces a reaction. The curtain call at the end of the performance is perhaps the best example of this type of elicitor. Although hints of the characters they played often linger in their personas, the actors openly acknowledge their roles as performers in the game of theatre, and the audience often revels in its chance to congratulate them for their successful artistry. When spectatorial knowledge of an actor's stardom figures in her or his response during a performance, the social mode is also primary.

As previously noted, spectators move in and out of the blend at every performance, and their moment-to-moment emotions may be keyed as much by a social as by a dramatic response. Oftentimes, theatre artists induce spectators to alter their previous reaction to a fictitious figure, either through social or dramatic means or a combination of both. This change is what Feagin calls a "meta-response." A metaresponse involves a spectator's rethinking and rejection of her or his earlier response, from whatever source. Brecht deployed metaresponse frequently in *Mother Courage*, often to call attention to the contradictions between Courage as a caring mother and as a hyena of the battlefield. For most spectators one of the most memorable instances of metaresponse probably occurred when they were invited to contrast the end of scene 6 with the start of scene 7. After Kattrin is disfigured and Courage realizes that her daughter will never get a husband or her own children, Courage says, "It's the war that made her dumb too; a soldier stuffed something in her mouth when she was little. I'll never see Swiss Cheese again and where Elif is, God knows. God damn the war." When scene 7 begins, however, Courage, wearing a necklace of silver coins, tells the Chaplain, "Stop running down the war. I won't have it. I know it destroys the weak, but the weak haven't a chance in peacetime either. And war is a better provider." Then she launches into a song praising the business of war. Above her, Brecht's sign for the scene read, "Mother Courage at the height of her business career."[24]

As this example suggests, metaresponse always involves a two-step reversal. First, spectators are lulled into one emotion at either the dramatic or social level and then abruptly forced to reject that response when new information slaps them in the face. In the above example, many spectators may have momentarily believed that Courage had learned something from her experiences, agreed with her "damn the war" statement, and even sympathized with her for her pain. In the next instant, though, spectators probably rejected their first response and condemned her for her rapaciousness and her indifference to suffering. Brecht peppered his production with several inducements for metaresponse. In the final scene Weigel-Courage, desolate over the death of Kattrin, fished a few coins out of her purse to pay the peasants to bury her daughter but put one coin back and snapped her purse shut before giving the peasants the rest. This likely led to the same two-step reversal for the audience, prompted in this case by her business-sense frugality, checking her financial generosity in the face of Kattrin's death.

Brecht understood the effect that metaresponse could have on his audience and even spoke at times about Verfremdungseffekt as a kind of metaresponse. The playwright-director believed that the initial consequence of the effect of alienation on an audience would be momentary *Befremdung* (bewilderment). The familiar has been made strange, and spectators, caught off guard, will not know what to make of it. In Brecht's formulation this bewilderment prepares the way for new insights and even possible actions. As Brecht scholar Reinhold Grimm explains, Brecht understood this as a triadic process—from contentment with the normal, to bewilderment about its strangeness, to an insight that the normal must be transformed. Grimm points out that this was a Hegelian process for Brecht: "Our initial, both imperfect and incomplete, comprehension equals a Hegelian thesis; this gives way, if only temporarily, to a total incomprehension equaling a Hegelian antithesis; and this, in turn, provokes the final and genuine comprehension, which is tantamount to a Hegelian synthesis or a Hegelian 'sublation' (*Aufhebung*), in the triple sense of negation, preservation, and elevation to a higher level."[25]

It is clear that the first two steps in this process, from contentment to bewilderment, are essentially the same as the two-step reversal of

Feagin's metaresponse. And it is likely that many spectators experienced this while watching *Mother Courage*. Feagin would agree with Brecht that the first two steps can prepare the way for the transformation of the third, but that they must lead to a higher insight appears to be cognitively problematic. Metaresponse certainly induces what might be called "second thoughts" in spectators, but this does not mean that they will necessarily reach Brecht's conclusion that history must be transformed so that the normal can accord with the utopian.

Other playwrights have used metaresponse to advantage in their dramatic rhetoric, but it is probably fair to say that most have not understood the two-step reversal of metaresponse as a springboard into the three-step process of audience transformation through Hegelian dialectic. David Rabe, however, deployed the surprise of metaresponse to provoke the dialectical process of understanding, much like Brecht. Interestingly, though, he used a Brechtian-like dialectic in *Streamers* to move his audience toward a very un-Brechtian stance against war.[26]

In many ways *Streamers* (1977) is the opposite of *Mother Courage*. Climactic in structure rather than episodic, entirely realist in style instead of a mix of several stylistic modes, and awash in what Brecht would have regarded as empathy and emotion, *Streamers* nevertheless deploys two-step metaresponse to achieve many of its major effects and possible meanings. Rabe does this by keeping his audience in the dark about the intentions and vulnerabilities of his major characters. As they await their orders to ship out for Vietnam, his three young males play at army duties, test each other for signs of racism and homosexuality, and attempt to form friendships, all within the constraints of an army bunkhouse. Into this tenuous, emerging situation rages Carlyle, a human grenade angry about being drafted—and a person, the audience comes to believe, who will explode before the play is over. (Carlyle is a new version of the pistol-over-the-mantelpiece convention; hearing that he is effectively "loaded" in act 1, the audience knows he will be "fired" before the play is over.) Sure enough, by the end of the action, Carlyle has killed Billy, a young recruit, and Rooney, an old sergeant who stumbles into the dramatic situation at the wrong place and the wrong time.

Indeed, accidents, coupled with ignorance, are the keys to the play's structure and its use of metaresponse and dialectical rhetoric. For most of *Streamers* Rabe keeps the audience and the other characters in the dark about Richie's homosexuality, about the depth of Billy's homophobia, about the desires of Carlyle, and about other information that leads to the killings at the end. This results in several situations in which the audience takes sides with one character only to discover a moment later that that person has badly misjudged another character and the general situation. Spectators often sympathize with Billy, for example, usually the most well-intentioned of the characters, but are soon jolted into the recognition that his innocence has blinded him to some crucial knowledge about himself or others. As in *Mother Courage,* metaresponse opens up *Streamers* for potential audience insight. Because characters in both plays remain largely ignorant of their historical situation and of the repetitions that bind their actions, the audience is challenged to place the Billys and Courages of both into a larger context to make sense of their lives. The bewilderment caused by metaresponse induces spectators to think against the grain. Confronted by their misplaced sympathies, audiences must struggle for meaning; both plays invite them to move from bewilderment to insight.

Arguably, Rabe gave the audience more help than Brecht. The German playwright-director complained that many spectators ended up admiring Weigel's Mother Courage because she persevered during difficult times despite the loss of her children. (No doubt many spectators identified with Courage in 1949 because they, too, had lost children during the war. Drawing on contemporary comments and reviews, historian John Fuegi concludes that the 1949 audience sat "in stunned and mesmerized silence broken only by the sound of their own sobbing.")[27] These spectators, said Brecht, had missed the point of the play, which he stated forthrightly in his model book: "That in wartime the big profits are not made by little people. That war, which is a continuation of business by other means, makes the human virtues fatal even to their possessors. That no sacrifice is too great for the struggle against war."[28]

While it is likely that some spectators did put the pieces of the play together to make those or similar meanings, Brecht supplied no sympathetic figure in *Mother Courage* to lead audience members toward this synthesis. Rabe, in contrast, gave the audience Sergeant Cokes at the end of the play, whose rambling story about a car crash setting off a string of other accidents provided an encapsulating metaphor for the absurdity of war and an appropriate coda for *Streamers.* Where Brecht pointed to capitalism as the underlying cause of war, Rabe wanted his spectators to be appalled by its absurdity but offered no general explanation of its cause.

Brecht and Rabe used different theatrical means to point their audiences toward very different conclusions about warfare, but both deployed metaresponse and dialectical rhetoric to get them there. Despite Brecht's worries that theatrical realism would naturalize the world and inhibit historical change, Rabe, like Brecht, deployed a two-step reversal that could knock spectators out of their unexamined sympathies and prompt the third step of progressive thought, even in a realist play.

Clearly, this aspect of Verfremdungseffekt is not unique to Brechtian theatre.[29]

Notes

1. Ralph Manheim and John Willett, eds., *Bertolt Brecht: Collected Plays,* vol. 5 (New York: Random House, 1972). This volume contains Brecht's *Mother Courage and Her Children* (133–210) and "The Mother Courage Model" [1956] (334–86).

2. See Gilles Fauconnier and Mark Turner, *The Way We Think: Conceptual Blending and the Mind's Hidden Complexities* (New York: Basic Books, 2002), 217–67.

3. Ibid., 267.

4. See Kendall Walton, *Mimesis as Make-Believe: On the Foundations of the Representational Arts* (Cambridge, MA: Harvard University Press, 1990).

5. See Erving Goffman, *Frame Analysis* (Garden City, NY: Doubleday, 1974).

6. Brecht, "Mother Courage Model," 336.

7. Ibid., 338.

8. John Rouse, *Brecht and the West German Theatre* (Ann Arbor, MI: UMI Research Press, 1989), 29. See also Elin Diamond's comments on Brechtian theatre in her *Unmaking Mimesis* (London: Routledge, 1997).

9. Brecht, "Mother Courage Model," 335.

10. Ibid., 379.

11. See Susan Feagin, *Reading with Feeling: The Aesthetics of Appreciation* (Ithaca, NY: Cornell University Press, 1996), 113–39.

12. See Terry Eagleton, *The Ideology of the Aesthetic* (Cambridge, MA: Basil Blackwell, 1990), 31–69.

13. Robert M. Gordon, "Simulation, Sympathy, and the Impartial Spectator," in *Mind and Morals: Essays on Cognitive Science and Ethics,* ed. Larry May, Marilyn Friedman, and Andy Clark (Cambridge, MA: MIT Press, 1996), 165–80.

14. Antonio Damasio, *Looking for Spinoza: Joy, Sorrow, and the Feeling Brain* (New York: Harcourt, 2003), 116, 118.

15. Georg Vielmetter, "The Theory of Holistic Simulation: Beyond Interpretivism and Postempiricism," in *Empathy and Agency: The Problem of Understanding in the Human Sciences,* ed. Hans Herbert Kogler and Karsten R. Steuber (Boulder, CO: Westview Press, 2000), 95.

16. Gordon, "Simulation," 165–68, 168.

17. Brecht, *Mother Courage,* 135.

18. Gordon, "Simulation," 168.

19. For an example of Ekman's work see Paul Ekman, "Facial Expressions of Emotion: New Findings, New Questions," *Psychological Science* 3 (1992): 34–38.

20. Brecht, "Mother Courage Model," 353, 358, 356, 359.

21. Ibid., 362.

22. George Steiner, *The Death of Tragedy* (New York: Knopf, 1958), 348.

23. Feagin, *Reading with Feeling*, 5–87.

24. Brecht, *Mother Courage*, 184, 185.

25. Reinhold Grimm, "Alienation in Context: On the Theory and Practice of Brechtian Theatre," in *A Bertolt Brecht Reference Companion*, ed. Siegfried Mews (Westport, CT: Greenwood Press, 1997), 42.

26. David Rabe, *Streamers* [1977], in *The Vietnam Plays*, vol. 2 (New York: Grove Press, 1993), 1–84. See also Rabe's "Afterword: 1992" in the same volume, 181–97.

27. John Fuegi, *Bertolt Brecht: Chaos according to Plan* (Cambridge, UK: Cambridge University Press, 1987), 123.

28. Brecht, "Mother Courage Model," 339.

29. Although Brecht believed that realism and his V-effect were antithetical, he did acknowledge that Verfremdungseffekt was not unique to epic theatre. In 1955 he wrote to Henri Magnan: "Alienation effects have long been known in the theatre and in other arts. The fact is that we always get an alienation effect when art does not sustain the illusion that the viewer is face-to-face with nature itself. In the theatre, for instance, the objective world is alienated by the convention of versification or by a highly personal style or by abrupt shifts between verse and prose or between the serious and the comic" (John Willett, ed., *Bertolt Brecht Letters*, trans. Ralph Manheim [London: Methuen, 1990], 543).

Porgy and Bess as Propaganda

Preaching to the [Eva Jessye] Choir

Alan Woods

THE NOTION THAT performance can serve as propaganda dates back to the earliest recorded history of performance; we read that the City Dionysia festival in fifth-century BCE Athens served, at least in part, to impress the allies and opponents alike of the Athenian Empire with Attica's cultural prowess. Medieval cities strove to outdo each other with religious performances and festivals, and local notables in Renaissance Italy took advantage of the new technology of the printing press to make sure that lavish accounts of their equally lavish celebrations were in the hands of rival dukes, and city councils were equally quick to publicize the sumptuousness of their welcoming the entries of touring monarchs.

These examples of performance as propaganda from European history tend to fall into the category of those events intended to impress others. There is yet another variation on the propaganda theme: the use of performance to both impress and, equally important from the point of view of those aiming to gain advantage from performance, to change the perceptions of audiences about the society that produced the performance in question—the move, if you will, from relatively simple impression to a change in attitude. How effective are such efforts? An episode from early in the cold war may provide some useful insights both into how attempts at theatre-as-propaganda are created and into their general effectiveness.

The United States government's first major effort to employ performance art for political and propaganda purposes overseas came after World War II, as the Iron Curtain clanked into place and the cold war era began.[1] Cultural exchange was quickly perceived as a viable weapon in that cold war, especially after the ecstatic response earned during the first European tour of Ballet Theatre (renamed the American Ballet Theatre for the occasion) in 1950 and 1951. The ABT tour was under the auspices of a newly revitalized American National Theatre and Academy (ANTA) and was produced by ANTA's first executive director, Robert Breen, and the ABT board president, Blevins Davis. Although the ABT was not under official government sponsorship, Breen managed to get the military to transport the company to Europe free in exchange for free performances at U.S. Army camps in Germany. (According to Breen he managed this by answering a general's query, "What's the Ballet Theatre?" with "it's just a bunch of pretty girls in pink tights.")[2]

There is not space here to detail the as-yet-unwritten histories of Robert Breen's significant role in the early history of the nonprofit theatre of the United States[3] or to explore the fascinating career of Blevins Davis, an apparently charming rogue who amassed a fortune by a fortuitous and brief marriage—his elderly heiress bride had the good grace to die less than a year after the wedding.[4] Davis's influence was enhanced as well by the happy chance of his having been a childhood friend and neighbor of President Harry S. Truman. By late 1951 Breen and Davis saw an opportunity to mount a touring production of the Gershwin-Heyward *Porgy and Bess,* to do so inexpensively through the agency of ANTA's nonprofit, government-chartered status, and to cushion any losses by having the U.S. Department of State provide guarantees for selected overseas engagements in areas where the department thought the image of the United States could use some burnishing.[5]

Why *Porgy and Bess?* Breen later said it was because everywhere he'd traveled in Europe while he arranged the ABT tour, he heard people whistling or singing the Gershwin music.[6] The opera itself had a checkered career. Unsuccessful financially at its 1935 premiere, a highly praised 1938 revival on the West Coast bankrupted its producer. By contrast, Cheryl Crawford's 1942 Broadway revival—with spoken dialogue rather than the original recitative—enjoyed a nine-month run and an eighteen-month national tour, even though the Gershwin family denigrated it as "the cut-rate Porgy."[7] In various forms the work had been performed in some European opera houses (usually in blackface), although it had been banned by the Nazis as degenerate: it was, after all, by a Jewish composer and was about southern African Americans.

Porgy and Bess had also been recorded several times by 1951. Members of the original New York cast recorded some of the music, and opera stars Lawrence Tibbett and Helen Jepson recorded excerpts with the Metropolitan Opera orchestra in 1936. Goddard Lieberson produced the first "full-length" disk version in 1951, with Lehman Engle conducting.

Individual songs from the work, notably "Summertime," "It Ain't Necessarily So," and "Bess, You Is My Woman Now," had become popular standards, widely recorded in a variety of styles on both singles and albums. The music was widely known and admired—it wasn't just in Europe that one could expect to hear Gershwin's music on the street.

By late 1951 *Porgy and Bess* was also controversial. When DuBose Heyward wrote the novel *Porgy*, in 1925, it was widely regarded (and hailed) as a realistic depiction of southern black life, a depiction that shattered the condescending stereotypes in earlier works by white writers. The dramatization that Dorothy Heyward coauthored with her husband, produced on Broadway in 1927, gathered similar reactions, including praise from James Weldon Johnson of the NAACP, who, taking note of the production's more than sixty African American actors, observed that the production proved that black artists could perform serious roles with "thoughtful interpretation and intelligent skill."[8]

Attitudes were different in the early 1950s, as the civil rights movement gathered force. Rather than shattering stereotypes, *Porgy and Bess* was now regarded in some progressive circles as perpetuating them. Bess was, after all, a cocaine addict of uncertain virtue, and the inhabitants of Catfish Row were superstitious, ignorant, and easily misled. *Porgy and Bess* had become an emblem of shifting American attitudes regarding racism; indeed, in some quarters it was perceived as a clear example of racist attitudes.

Also different by the early 1950s was the availability of trained performers, one result of increased opportunities for African American artists. In 1927 the Theatre Guild had to rehearse *Porgy* for several months: its actors were drawn from vaudeville and musical comedy, since virtually no African American actors had the opportunity to do, let alone acquire experience in, serious drama in the commercial American theatre, and the Guild's casting net did not extend northward to the art theatres of Harlem. In 1935 casting the opera had required scouring church choirs along the eastern seaboard to find sufficient numbers of skilled singers. Casting in 1952 was easier: the Breen-Davis cast came from Juilliard, Ohio's Karamu House and the Cleveland Institute of Music, the Curtis Institute in Philadelphia, and other prestigious venues. Breen was able to cast performers prepared for careers in the concert hall and in opera (although not yet, in 1952, in any American opera houses).

The controversy surrounding *Porgy and Bess* both attracted and dismayed the State Department. Official U.S. sponsorship would obviously countermand Soviet publicity about racial segregation and the degrading conditions of life in the United States for most African Americans: if the opera was perceived as a celebration of African American life by one of America's best-known (and popular) composers, its very presentation could indicate the willingness of a democratic society to air its problems. However, it could also be argued that the opera was demeaning, not only for its reinscription of vicious stereotypes emerging from Heyward's benignly paternalistic racism but also through Gershwin's co-option of authentic African musical motifs and patterns, stolen from the Gullah culture of South Carolina and turned into slick, commercial music. From this perspective the U.S. government's sponsorship of *Porgy and Bess* would validate a long-standing cultural imperialism, in which African American performing arts and performing artists were swallowed up by a white commercial establishment, then regurgitated in sanitized white-faced versions that destroyed the original's vitality.

This controversy was not resolved in 1951, and it was only partly settled by the work's achieving iconic status with the Metropolitan Opera's belated production of *Porgy and Bess* in 1985.[9] The protests were muted in 1951, and, no doubt helped by Blevins Davis's White House connections, the State Department agreed to cover any losses from the opera's engagements in Vienna and West Berlin in September and October 1952. The Breen-Davis production, presented under the auspices of their newly formed nonprofit group, the Everyman Opera Company, opened in Dallas in July 1952. After playing in Chicago, Cleveland, and Washington, DC, the sixty-five performers and fifteen support staff were flown to Vienna in military transport aircraft. Heading the cast were newlyweds William Warfield and Leontyne Price, with Cab Calloway as Sportin' Life, playing for the first time the role written for him by the Gershwins. The redoubtable Eva Jessye trained and led the chorus, as she had with each production since 1935. Alexander Smallens was musical director, also repeating from the original production, and central to the decision to restore music cut earlier and to present *Porgy and Bess* as an opera.

The response in both Vienna and West Berlin was rapturous. Not only was the production itself praised by local critics and enormously popular with audiences (in both cities all seats were sold out in a few hours after the opening), the production's cast and staff took their roles as goodwill ambassadors extremely seriously, attending embassy parties and social events, entertaining almost anywhere, virtually on demand.[10] The response was so positive that the United States Information Agency produced a short film to be shown in Europe and elsewhere overseas to further exploit the propaganda value of the opera's tour.

The offstage activities of the *Porgy and Bess* performers, it turned out, were an unexpected propaganda bonus. Although the State Department had been worried about the impact of the production's plot, characterizations, and potentially negative stereotyping, it had not considered the effect the cast members would create. These were, after all, classically trained and highly skilled artists—William Warfield stunned audiences in Vienna, for example, when he gave a benefit concert during the *Porgy and Bess* run there, singing German *lieder* with a flawless accent. And because Breen had insisted on doubling all the major roles, to ensure that voices were fresh at each performance, many European audiences, confronted for the first time with African American singers of operatic quality, saw an apparently endless array of talented, sophisticated, and stylishly dressed singers from an America depicted in much of their media as a land of lynchings.[11]

The actions of the *Porgy and Bess* cast quickly became major events in each city, with massive press coverage. Black mannequins appeared in fashionable shop windows in both Vienna and Berlin, for example. In divided Berlin, pre-Wall, currency from the Soviet sector began to appear in the box office at the Titania Palast Theatre; even though it was not normally accepted in the western sectors, the State Department quickly agreed to reimburse the theatre, so great was the propaganda value of attracting East Berliners to the capitalistic American opera. When *Porgy and Bess* returned to the United States, to open at the Ziegfeld Theatre in New York in March 1953 (after playing Paris and London, without government support), its success had encouraged the new president, Dwight Eisenhower, to request an annual appropriation of five million dollars from Congress for cultural exchange programs, half of which was earmarked for theatrical productions. Eisenhower also wrote a letter for the New York souvenir program, stating (in part), "I cannot emphasize too strongly how serious and enduring this work seems to me. You and your company are making a real contribution to the kind of understanding between nations that alone can bring mutual respect and trust."[12] Blevins Davis had solicited the Eisenhower letter, through Bernard Baruch; even so, the letter reflected the role theatrical productions were to play in cultural exchanges for the next two decades, which saw an increasing willingness by the federal government to underwrite foreign tours of American art as part of the propaganda effort to offset Soviet successes on cultural, military, and scientific fronts.

After playing 305 performances in New York (the longest run of any *Porgy and Bess* production to date), the Breen-Davis company toured the United States and then later in 1954 returned to Europe. The State Department once again guaranteed performances, this time in Zagreb, Belgrade, Alexandria, Cairo, Athens, Tel Aviv, Casablanca, and Barcelona. The earlier successes were repeated, both onstage and off; in Cairo cast members met President Gamal Abdel-Nasser, and in Tel Aviv Israelis anxious to see the production sat in the aisles when all seats were sold.

In Athens the production was credited with thwarting an anti-American propaganda campaign started by communist sympathizers. Joseph James, who sang Jake, noted that many company members routinely learned songs in local languages to sing at receptions throughout the tour.[13]

The State Department also sponsored a *Porgy and Bess* tour to South America in the summer and early fall of 1955, with the production again selling out theatres, receiving positive reviews, and cast members doing double duty as goodwill ambassadors. But when the Soviet government invited *Porgy and Bess* to perform in Leningrad (now St. Petersburg) and Moscow late in 1955, the State Department refused to support the tour, also rejecting Breen's request for visas to perform for sixteen weeks in mainland China, at Beijing's invitation. The Soviet government stepped into the breech and subsidized the company in Russia, presumably happy to reinforce the idea that the Soviet system supported African American artists more than their own government, which was at the same time restricting the travel and career of Paul Robeson, well-known to Russian audiences.[14] Thus, on December 26, 1955, *Porgy and Bess* opened in Leningrad under Soviet, not American, auspices—the first American theatrical production to play in Russia after World War II.[15]

After some minor problems,[16] the opera was greeted with its usual wild enthusiasm in both Russian cities—and with lavish parties and receptions hosted by American ambassador Charles Bohlen, the American government apparently having decided to take advantage of the opera's presence (and the enormous publicity it engendered on both sides of the Iron Curtain), even if it refused financial support.

Porgy and Bess went on to play Prague, Warsaw, and Stalinogród (now Katowice), Poland, without U.S. support; Breen and Davis were refused permission to accept an invitation from Bulgaria. The production went on to West Germany, the Netherlands, Norway, and Denmark, finally closing in Amsterdam on June 3, 1956.

As cultural propaganda, *Porgy and Bess* sent a decidedly mixed message: an undisputed classic of American musical theatre, for many critics it reinscribed harshly negative stereotypes in its characters, plot settings, and language. Furthermore, it transformed authentic African-based music into a commercial product. The opera could therefore be seen as a prime example of cultural imperialism.

Porgy and Bess also, however, demonstrated vividly to European, South American, and North African audiences that African Americans had access to skilled vocal and dramatic training in sufficient numbers to populate a large production and that the American theatre could produce a moving and theatrically exciting operatic performance. African American performers on the tour behaved as freewheeling and highly sophisticated individual artists, clearly not the victims of grinding debasement institutionalized by a dominant white society—indeed, Ambassador Bohlen wrote in his memoirs that the actors' insistence on wandering "out alone" generated complaints from Soviet authorities, who found the actors' desire for ready access to Soviet citizens unnerving.[17] It is ironic that members of the *Porgy and Bess* company experienced racial slurs and segregation during their four-year tour not in Europe, northern Africa, or South America but in parts of the United States, even though the production avoided an American South still segregated in the mid-1950s.[18]

The government supported "safer" theatrical productions after *Porgy and Bess,* including an ANTA revival of *The Skin of Our Teeth,* with Helen Hayes and Mary Martin in Paris (1955), and a Soviet tour for *My Fair Lady* in 1960. The controversies *Porgy and Bess* spawned also foreshadowed later efforts by some governmental leaders to monitor the content of federally supported art. Although enormously successful, both artistically and as American propaganda, therefore, *Porgy and Bess* epitomizes the uncertainty of exporting performances as a governmental tool. The multiple messages the production sent, many of them unanticipated by either the State Department or the opera's creative team, made it impossible to control audience response and, thus, to forecast precisely its impact.

But what of its overall effectiveness as propaganda? As I've indicated, *Porgy and Bess* had both unexpected and expected consequences. It was undoubtedly effective as a theatrical venture and also highly effective in the impact company members had individually in the cities where they toured. I would argue, however, that the larger hope for the production's propaganda purposes, to enhance the perception of the United States as a free democracy in opposition to the Soviet system of repression, was not achieved in any appreciable measure. The production of *Porgy and Bess* did, after all, literally preach to the choir: to an educated audience of relatively sophisticated theatregoers, many of whom were already familiar with the opera's score. And despite the many accounts of large, enthusiastic audiences, the opera was, after all, performed in cultural centers and in facilities identified with a relatively narrow segment of the cultural elite. *Porgy and Bess* did not, in fact, play to mass audiences.

There is an additional problem with the very notion of performance as propaganda, at least in the context of what was, after all, a traditional theatrical tour, organized in the context of the Western commercial entertainment industry. Breen's entire concept of theatre was set by the industrial standards; although his pioneering work at ANTA set the stage for, and prefigured many of the practices of, the not-for-profit theatre that would emerge a decade or so later, his *Porgy and Bess* tour is indistinguishable from any purely commercial tour of the period; the State Department subventions and the various other sponsorships of the tour served to reach the tour's break-even point.

The *Porgy and Bess* tour, in short, was part of the commodity theatre. That theatre is essentially passive: it reinforces the views of its audiences, since that is how those audiences are attracted to purchase seats to the entertainment event. The commercial commodity theatre is not designed to startle, shock, or upset its audience, as Brecht and Piscator recognized some eight decades ago. Like its more manifestly commercial counterparts, *Porgy and Bess* was not written or produced in a context to persuade or to present new examinations of African American social life but served rather to reinforce already extant perceptions in its audiences.

There were attempts, with varying degrees of success, in the immediate post–World War II era to find ways in which performance could be employed for social or political ends; Jean Vilar's continuing the efforts of the Théâtre National Populaire in France, during the same years that *Porgy and Bess* was playing in Paris, comes to mind, as does the work of Brecht himself at the Berliner Ensemble. But those efforts had to create new structures outside the commercial framework. The commodity-driven theatre is by its very nature antithetical to the didactic needs of propaganda, unless that propaganda is of the traditional, passive type that most commodity forms generally include: reinforcing the hegemonic normative at the expense of any innovative or disturbing elements. And as recent events in the Islamic world suggest, popular entertainment often can have a negative impact, as audiences can find some elements offensive, if not blasphemous.

The Breen-Davis *Porgy and Bess*, therefore, preached to the choir. The choir of the relatively affluent, traditionally cultured members of what we would now think of as the elites of their day. The production had little lasting political effect that I can discern, either in changing or reinforcing favorable views of American policies and programs or in counterbalancing the influence of the Soviet Union. Its most demonstrable impact, in fact, was literally on the choir—in this case the onstage choir, trained and conducted by Eva Jessye. The touring production of *Porgy and Bess* was, for many of its cast, a life-altering event; many went on to long and illustrious careers in American theatre, cinema, television, and opera. But there seems to have been no comparable effect on the production's audiences.

Notes

1. An early view of the values of cultural exchange is in Harold E. Snyder's *When Peoples Speak to Peoples* (Washington: American Council on Education, 1953); a somewhat more sophisticated approach is documented in *Cultural Affairs and Foreign Relations,* published by the American Assembly as a working document for its 1962 conference (Englewood Cliffs, NJ: Prentice-Hall, 1963). A more overtly doctrinaire position, applicable to the present case, is in V. Syrokomskii, comp., *The Truth about Cultural Exchange* (Moscow: Progress, 1977).

2. Wilva Davis Breen, interview by Lorraine Brown, Sep. 5, 1987, audiocassette C10, Oral History Archives, Jerome Lawrence and Robert E. Lee Theatre Research Institute, Ohio State University (cited hereafter as the Lawrence and Lee Institute).

3. Breen (1914–1990) began his career with the Federal Theatre Project in Chicago. His theatrical career was essentially over after the failure of *Free and Easy/Blues Opera* in 1960, the last venture of the Everyman Opera Company.

4. Davis (1903–1971) was president of the American Ballet Theatre, cofounder of the Cripple Creek (Colorado) District Museum, and had produced three Broadway plays prior to *Porgy and Bess.*

5. Breen was dismissed as executive director of ANTA early in 1951, in part because of conflicts with the board over plans to tour *Porgy and Bess.* With Davis he promptly organized the Everyman Opera Company to present the tour. The Breen-Davis tour of *Porgy and Bess* is treated in Hollis Alpert's *The Life and Times of Porgy and Bess* (New York: Knopf, 1990), 143–254. Alpert draws heavily on the Robert Breen Collection, Lawrence and Lee Institute, as well as on the Lawrence and Lee Institute's Oral History Archives, which contain interviews with many members of the *Porgy and Bess* cast.

6. Wilva Davis Breen, interview by Lorraine Brown, Sep. 3, 1987, audiocassette C9, Oral History Archives, Lawrence and Lee Institute.

7. Wilva Davis Breen, interview by Lorraine Brown, Aug. 8, 1987, audiocassette C1, Oral History Archives, Lawrence and Lee Institute.

8. As cited by Alpert, *Life and Times,* 67.

9. See Donal Henahan, "A Good Deed, but a Disservice to Gershwin," *New York Times,* March 10, 1985. For an example of the work's iconic status see Pierre Ruhe, "'Porgy and Bess,' Classics Ground Atlanta Opera for 'Safe' Season," *Atlanta Journal-Constitution,* Feb. 10, 2005. Continuing controversies surrounding the opera are covered by Barbara Zuck, "Changing Attitudes on Race Affect 'Porgy and Bess,'" *Columbus Dispatch,* Oct. 3, 2004.

10. Joseph Attles, one of several alternate Sportin' Lifes, frequently entertained at embassy parties, as did many others of the cast; see Joseph Attles, interview by Alan Woods, Dec. 12, 1987, audiocassette C28, Oral History Archives, Lawrence and Lee Institute.

11. Some of the more informal interactions between cast members and the general public are amusingly recounted by Maya Angelou, who joined the production for its second European tour in 1954, in her third volume of auto-

biography, *Singin' and Swingin' and Gettin' Merry like Christmas* (New York: Bantam Books, 1977).

12. *Porgy and Bess* souvenir program, Program File, Lawrence and Lee Institute.

13. Joseph James, interview by Alan Woods, Dec. 13, 1987, audiocassette C33, Oral History Archives, Lawrence and Lee Institute.

14. For the controversies surrounding Robeson's contacts with the Soviet Union, a useful summary is in Martin Duberman, *Paul Robeson: A Biography* (New York: New Press, 1989), esp. 415–19. A harsher recent view is presented in Eric Breindel's *New York Post* column of July 31, 1997, reprinted as "Paul Robeson and Soviet Jewry," in *A Passion for Truth: The Selected Writings of Eric Breindel,* ed. John Podhoretz (New York: HarperCollins, 1999), 54–57.

15. Truman Capote accompanied the tour to the Soviet Union, ostensibly to write an article for the *New Yorker* magazine. His articles, which, after appearing in the magazine, were published in book form as *The Muses Are Heard* (New York: Random House, 1956), provide an entertaining, if biased and fundamentally inaccurate, account of the venture.

16. The official speeches and welcoming ceremonies delayed the curtain for over an hour at the first Leningrad performance; also, the printed programs were not ready for the first performance, leaving the Russian audience a bit mystified about the plot until a translator read a plot synopsis during the intermission.

17. Charles E. Bohlen, *Witness to History, 1929–1969* (New York: Norton, 1973).

18. Numerous incidents are reported in the interviews with *Porgy and Bess* cast members in the Lawrence and Lee Institute Oral History Archives: Lillian Hayman reports one typical example involving hotel accommodations in Columbus, Ohio, during 1954 (see Lillian Hayman, interview by Alan Woods, Dec. 16, 1987, audiocassette C24), and Howard Roberts describes difficulties with restaurants in California (see Howard Roberts, interview by Alan Woods, July 23, 1992, audiocassette C300).

Inventing the Heartland

The Theatre Guild, *Oklahoma!* and World War II

Claudia Wilsch Case

W HEN THE THEATRE GUILD staged *Oklahoma!* in 1943, it cemented the Guild's position as the premiere producing organization in America. Founded shortly after World War I, the Theatre Guild had already gone through several transformations, each of which allowed it to grow and influence a generation of American theatre. The Guild was instrumental in changing the Broadway stage from a place cluttered with revues, farces, and melodramas into a home for artistic and intellectual drama.

In its early years the Theatre Guild introduced contemporary European plays to New York, notably staging American premieres of the works of George Bernard Shaw, and it established relationships with skilled actors, producing a series of hit shows that displayed the talents of Alfred Lunt and Lynn Fontanne. During the mid-to-late 1920s the Guild's producers turned their attention to plays by American writers, forging a bond with Eugene O'Neill and encouraging the work of up-and-coming playwrights such as Sidney Howard and S. N. Behrman. By 1939 control of the Theatre Guild passed from a six-member board of directors into the hands of Guild founder Lawrence Langner and executive director Theresa Helburn, who balanced their desire to bring sophisticated plays to the stage with a concern for financial return.

Nowhere are the Theatre Guild's simultaneous artistic and commercial interests more evident than in its production of *Oklahoma!* The work on which the musical is based, Lynn Riggs's 1931 folk play *Green Grow the Lilacs,* had been only a modest success for the Guild during the Depression, when its nostalgic but blunt depiction of hardscrabble life in turn-of-the-century Indian Territory spoke to a need for Americans to be resilient during difficult times. When Theresa Helburn was watching a revival of the play at Langner's Westport Country Playhouse in the summer of 1940, she reimagined *Green Grow the Lilacs* as a musical. Helburn believed that the wholesome midwestern setting and its characters, taken from an American past teeming with pioneer spirit, might hearten a nation headed for war. "We thought this was an ideal time to do a musical play about America," Helburn said, "and we wanted to recapture that special American flavor in the original script."[1]

The traditional story of *Oklahoma!* is that by integrating its plot, songs, and dances, Richard Rodgers and Oscar Hammerstein, together with Agnes de Mille and Rouben Mamoulian, revolutionized American musical theatre. This account is mostly accurate, but there is another story of the show's creation beneath the surface.[2] It is the story of how *Oklahoma!* changed not only the American musical but also America's perception of itself. The adaptation of *Green Grow the Lilacs* transformed Riggs's original in structure as well as in content, affirming traditional American values and conveying a message of optimism to a nation plunging into war. By changing *Green Grow the Lilacs* into *Oklahoma!* the Theatre Guild transformed the Dust Bowl into the heartland, the spiritual center of America from which the rest of the country could draw strength. In doing so, the producers were of course keying in to commercial considerations, but they were also contributing to an American mythology that would endure long after closing night.

Riggs's *Green Grow the Lilacs,* presented on Broadway in 1931, is the tragicomic story of Curly McClain, a plains cowboy, and Jeeter Fry, a farmhand, vying for the love of the farm girl Laurey Williams in the Indian Territory of the year 1900. A raucous "shivoree" celebrating the wedding of Laurey and Curly results in a jealous confrontation that leads to Jeeter's death, and the play closes on a looming trial for Curly. Given the producers' limited experience with musicals—they had previously staged only a handful, including *Porgy and Bess* in 1935—and given the rustic theme of Riggs's play, the project of adapting *Green Grow the Lilacs* into musical form was quite a departure from the Guild's record of producing sophisticated and intellectual work on Broadway.[3] Moreover, the undertaking proved financially difficult since the Theatre Guild's funds had been depleted by a recent series of failures. Numerous potential backers declined to invest in "plays about farm hands," and soon the project became known throughout New York's theatre circles as "Helburn's Folly."[4]

Undeterred, the Guild moved forward. To create the music, lyrics, and book for their new version of *Green Grow the Lilacs,* Helburn and

Langner hired Richard Rodgers and Oscar Hammerstein for their first collaboration. The songs Rodgers and Hammerstein wrote as they adapted Riggs's work emerge effortlessly from the book, explore the play's characters and themes, and propel the action forward.[5] Agnes de Mille's dances, which are cleverly woven into the music and dialogue, also move the plot along and elucidate its characters and themes. The choreographer, who had "made a very deep study of American folk material," had "become something of a specialist in this field" and wanted to revive and develop dance forms native to America within the framework of ballet.[6] As a result of de Mille's work on *Oklahoma!* ballet would ultimately lose its flavor of an imported European art form and become accepted in America as an indigenous mode of expression. For classically trained dancers like Joan McCracken and Bambi Linn, *Oklahoma!* provided a bridge to Broadway and a springboard for careers in musical theatre. Director Rouben Mamoulian, whom Langner and Helburn had picked for "his ability to handle folk material," a skill he had demonstrated when directing *Porgy and Bess,* saw to it that the transitions between dialogue, song, and dance flowed seamlessly.[7] Because of monetary constraints and negative responses from stars, the Theatre Guild cast largely unknown performers in the musical.[8] When they signed on to play the roles of Curly, Laurey, and Ado Annie, actors Alfred Drake, Joan Roberts, and Celeste Holm were in the early stages of their careers. *Oklahoma!* would launch them to fame, exemplifying the American credo that a combination of talent and hard work can lead to success.

While maneuvering within the tight confines of the producers' budget and facing wartime shortages of materials, set designer Lemuel Ayers and costume designer Miles White created a midwestern world onstage that presented a stylized bucolic idyll. Theresa Helburn points out that Ayers's economical backdrops were "praised almost as genre paintings of the American West," as they "caught at once the clear blue blaze of sky," the "hot yellow sunshine," and "the shade of wheat and tall corn" that suggested the wide expanse of the American frontier. Helburn further recalls that White, as he was designing period costumes for the production, "managed to turn out a set of trousseaux prettier than any 1900 Oklahoma belle ever dreamed of." By working with limited resources and even deliberately cutting some embellishments from the actors' costumes, the Theatre Guild not only emphasized the perceived beautiful simplicity of life in turn-of-the-century America but also demonstrated to wartime audiences that a little can go a long way.[9]

As Hammerstein and Rodgers were crafting their adaptation of *Green Grow the Lilacs,* they confronted some dark aspects of the script that posed particular problems for the potential success of a musical. Helburn points out the "rough cowboy 'shivoree'"—a noisy and vulgar serenade that occurs on Laurey and Curly's wedding night—Curly's possible "murder" of Jeeter, and his subsequent trial, as well as the play's "unhappy ending" as passages that needed revision.[10] A comparison of the original script and Hammerstein's libretto shows that Hammerstein softened the troubling aspects of Riggs's play and transformed the original ambiguous ending into a hopeful one. He also tightened the plot, further developed and added some characters and situations, and emphasized the humor in this bittersweet tale. As a result of these alterations the play reemerged as a patriotic piece of wartime propaganda that confirmed the belief of Americans in the spirit and resilience of their country.

In *Green Grow the Lilacs* America's energy is symbolized by the character of Laurey, but hers is a raw strength that needs to mature. In his depiction of Laurey, Riggs paints a candid portrait of an adolescent girl who is inexperienced and capricious. While she disguises her genuine fondness for the fresh-faced cowboy Curly, Laurey is unable to reject—and possibly secretly fascinated by—Jeeter, the lecherous farmhand who lives in a dingy smokehouse on her property. Despite her stated aversion to Jeeter, Laurey has agreed to accompany him to a "play party," and, fearful Jeeter might harm her if she does not go with him, Laurey turns down Curly when he invites her to be his date for the same event.

Hammerstein left Laurey's enigmatic character intact and collaborated with de Mille on making the girl's problematic decision whether to favor Curly or Jeeter (called Jud in the musical) a central theme. To accomplish this goal, Hammerstein added an "Elixir of Egypt," a potion that is supposed to help people make up their minds, to the trinkets the peddler sells Laurey.[11] The girl's partaking of this elixir and her falling asleep set the scene for an exploration of her subconscious, which is dramatized in de Mille's ballet "Laurey Makes Up Her Mind." As dancers take over for the actors onstage, Laurey imagines her wedding to Curly, but, in a shocking development, she ends up married to Jud. In Laurey's nightmare Jud shoots and kills Curly and triumphantly carries Laurey off, presumably to "rape" her, as can be gleaned from de Mille's choreographic notes for the musical's film adaptation.[12] De Mille conceived of this ballet for the end of act 1 to give expression to Laurey's fear of Jud and to motivate her sudden decision in act 2 to marry Curly. "This is the heart of Laurie's [*sic*] terror," the choreographer says of what she wanted to represent in the ballet. "This is where she's forced to make a decision, and the whole rest of the play is different because of this decision."[13] In both Riggs's and Hammerstein's versions Laurey's maturation into adulthood mirrors the transition of Indian Territory into statehood, and her marriage to Curly parallels the entry of the state of Oklahoma into the Union. On a deeper level the couple's marriage and the protection it grants Laurey from Jud must have presented a reassuring picture of stability to 1940s audiences, who were facing the threat and uncertainty of war.

While Hammerstein reinforced Riggs's characterization of Laurey, he transformed the character of Ado Annie Carnes quite strikingly. In *Green Grow the Lilacs* Annie is portrayed as the laughingstock of the community—a timid, "unattractive, stupid-looking" country bumpkin dressed in "very unbecoming" clothes—who tags along with Laurey to the "play party" because she can't find a date.[14] In Hammerstein's libretto, however, Ado Annie emerges as an attractive, clever, and flirtatious girl who has many men interested in her and simply "cain't say no" to any of them (*O* 28). Whereas Riggs's Annie is confused and overwhelmed as lusty boys proposition her at the party, Hammerstein's Annie is not intimidated by men, asserts herself as their equal, and explores her sexual freedom. She is much more independent and confident than the old Annie, and when she negotiates the terms of her marriage in her song "All er Nuthin," Hammerstein's Annie resembles in type the strong 1940s American women who demonstrated their capacity for self-reliance in America's wartime economy. Yet much like these women, who would eventually surrender their jobs to returning soldiers, Ado Annie gives up her independence when her intended, Will Parker, comes home from a trip to Kansas City.[15]

By making Will, a young cowboy who is only briefly mentioned in Riggs's script, into a full-fledged character and Annie's main love interest, and by expanding the role of the peddler, Hammerstein inserted a lighthearted subplot into Riggs's original story. Annie and Will function as comic foils to Laurey and Curly, and the foreign peddler, Ali Hakim, mirrors the outsider Jud, since he threatens Annie and Will's romantic relationship. Yet unlike the sleazy and violent Jud, who poses a serious menace to Laurey and Curly's well-being, the good-natured peddler is a rather unwilling hindrance to Annie's liaison with Will and ultimately helps bring about the young couple's wedding. In the end both rivals are safely eliminated—Jud by death and Ali Hakim by his marriage to Gertie Cummings, Laurey's former competitor for Curly's love—and order is restored all around.

Hammerstein derives much of the humor in his depiction of Annie and Will by framing their courtship in the quintessentially American concept of business. Annie's father, Andrew Carnes, gave Will his word he could marry his daughter should Will manage to produce fifty dollars. Having won such a sum at a rodeo, the ecstatic young man immediately spends the money on presents for his bride-to-be, unaware that only cold, hard cash will do for his prospective father-in-law. While Will was at the rodeo, Annie, who "didn't count on him bein' back so soon," got involved with the peddler, a sweet-talking man of questionable morals and business practices (O 25). Annie's father, suspicious that the foreigner may have compromised his daughter, insists he marry her. However, since he is a shrewd entrepreneur as well as a charmer, Ali Hakim manages to buy his freedom by helping Will regain the money he spent so quickly and thus making his rival attractive to the girl and her father once again. As soon as Will is able to show Annie's father the cash, Mr. Carnes's business instinct takes over and helps him select the most prosperous prospect for his daughter.

The theme of two men bartering for a bride is echoed and takes on a much more serious aspect in Hammerstein's depiction of Laurey and Curly's relationship. Hammerstein transformed Riggs's "play party" into a "box social," where women prepare picnic baskets that are auctioned off to raise money for a schoolhouse. During this event the women are not only judged by their cooking skills but also by their attractiveness to suitors and are thus metaphorically on the auction block themselves. When Laurey's basket comes up for sale, a grim bidding war erupts between the two rivals for her love, Curly and Jud. In the process of their confrontation each man parts with his most precious possessions: Jud puts up all the money he saved from two years of farm labor for the chance to win Laurey's basket, and Curly only manages to outbid him by liquidating the tools of his trade. To beat Jud's offer, Curly sells his saddle, his horse, and his gun to bystanders, thus dissolving his livelihood and his identity as a cowboy. Having raised the greater sum of money, Curly wins the girl.

Although Hammerstein generally softened the gloomier aspects of *Green Grow the Lilacs,* he inserted the dark auction scene into his libretto to emphasize the high stakes of Curly and Jud's competition for Laurey and the strength of character of the play's all-American hero. Curly's actions affirm American capitalism and ingenuity and at the same time emphasize the cowboy's integrity. With the funds he has procured through personal sacrifice, Curly not only invests in a bride but also in the greater good of the community—the construction of a schoolhouse. Hammerstein's newly created scene contributes dramatic tension and a well-positioned climax to the plot. By providing further motivation for Laurey to agree to marry Curly and by establishing a source for Jud's resentment and his subsequent revenge, the scene also pinpoints an important theme: the conflict between the cowboy and the farmer.

Although Indian Territory was presented onstage as an idyllic place that could make wartime audiences feel good about America vis-à-vis an unstable world, both *Green Grow the Lilacs* and *Oklahoma!* dramatize the tension between those characters who farm the land and those who use it as grazing ground for their cattle. Rodgers and Hammerstein illustrate this problem comically with their song "The Farmer and the Cowman Should Be Friends." Although the chorus tirelessly repeats the song's title lyrics and conveys a message of tolerance, sung and spoken interjections from the crowd seem to contradict this maxim by pointing out the ways in which cowboys and farmers continue to clash. An issue of particular contention is the farmers' building of fences "right across" the cowboys' "cattle ranges" (*O* 86). Fence building is a way of demarcating and protecting soil for cultivation and a symbol of the farmers' commitment to the land. The desire to tame nature goes along with the desire to civilize society, and greater social stability is the promise for the inhabitants of Indian Territory as they prepare to join the Union as the state of Oklahoma. In a world torn apart by war, these images of protection, cultivation, and civilization must have reminded American audiences of what their country was fighting for.

Riggs's play and Hammerstein's libretto are rich in indications that the settled farmers' way of life will ultimately prevail over that of the roaming cowboys as the territory approaches statehood. Curly, who starts out not being able to tell "a peach tree from a corn stalk," in time comes to realize, "Country a-changin', got to change with it!" By the end of the play he is ready to give up the itinerant life of the cowboy, settle down on Laurey's farm, begin tilling the soil, and become a citizen of the United States (*GGL* 61, 157; *O* 123). In a comical side note in Hammerstein's libretto, another peripatetic figure, the peddler, also puts down roots at the close of the play, although not entirely voluntarily. A shotgun wedding to one of the girls he has romanced has put an end to Ali Hakim's roving, and he is domesticated and coerced into running his father-in-law's store. Thus, the peddler, who used to travel "up and down and all around," is eventually absorbed into the community and assimilated into American culture (*O* 50).

Although Riggs specifies that the peddler is Syrian and Hammerstein describes him as Persian, in the Theatre Guild's production of *Oklahoma!* Ali Hakim was played by the Jewish comedian Joseph Buloff. The comic Jew was an old-established stereotype on the American stage, but this casting choice added political commentary to the production, emphasizing the notion that although Jews were being persecuted in Europe for their otherness, they formed an important part of American society.

Curly's conversion to farm life and the peddler's integration suggest that turn-of-the-century America valued stability, and the musical assured 1940s audiences that Americans could draw on the inherent strength of their country. The marriages that conclude the play not only signal social continuity but also convey to the audience a message of reconciliation of opposites. When the farm girl marries the cowboy, the hope that "territory folks should stick together" from the song "The Farmer and the Cowman" is realized, and the characters demonstrate that citizens of the United States should be loyal to each other and their country, especially in trying times (*O* 85). The simple lesson for contemporary audiences was that if Indian Territory could brave internal turmoil and shape itself into a state, the United States could overcome the adversities of an international war.

The characters in *Oklahoma!* look optimistically toward the future and the social and technological developments it brings. Both Riggs's and Hammerstein's scripts mention the people's excitement about Indian Territory's imminent transition to statehood, and Hammerstein's libretto heightens this anticipation with the song "Oklahoma," in which the characters celebrate the new name of their future state. It was not until the musical was in its Boston previews that its creators recognized the potential of this song as the "theme" for the show, expanded it with "one big chorus" sung by the entire cast, and decided to change the title of the musical—which up to this point had been *Away We Go*—to *Oklahoma!*[16] By developing "Oklahoma" into the theme song and committing to a new title, the Theatre Guild identified its musical fully with the American heartland.

In addition to emphasizing the social advancements of Indian Territory, *Oklahoma!* explores the inroads of modern technology into the turn-of-the-century Midwest. In his song "Everything's Up to Date in Kansas City" Will Parker enumerates the advances he has witnessed during his visit to the big city, such as automobiles, telephones, and skyscrapers, suggesting to 1940s audiences that America had been making great technological progress since the turn of the century and would continue to do so. The mechanical "two-step" and the fast "rag-time" Will demonstrates during his "Kansas City" song, along with the syncopated melody of the song "Oklahoma," echo the rhythm of industrial machinery and must have reminded contemporary audiences of the busy wartime industry that allowed the United States to prosper (*O* 17–19).

To give his libretto a message of optimism, Hammerstein developed many of the dark and ambiguous passages of Riggs's play into less-disturbing episodes by adding a dose of humor to the events. For example, he toned down the shivoree that pokes fun at the newly-weds' sexual initiation and proves to be psychologically traumatizing for Laurey. In *Green Grow the Lilacs* the men drag the couple outside and force them to climb atop a haystack, where they hurl "derisive and lascivious" language at them. Audiences and critics had complained about the impropriety of this scene when *Green Grow the Lilacs* was first staged, and the shivoree as Riggs had depicted it did not fit the healthy image of America that Rodgers and Hammerstein wanted to present. In his libretto Hammerstein cut this scene drastically and made certain to point out, "All are in high spirits. It is a good-natured hazing" (*GGL* 127; *O* 138).[17] Thus, rather than presenting the shivoree as an episode that disrupts the harmony between the newlyweds and the townspeople, the musical depicts it as an event that affirms the community's unity.

As in Riggs's play, when Jud arrives on the scene, intent on revenging his unrequited love for Laurey, the reveling turns deadly when he is killed in a fight with Curly. In this situation Laurey's fears of Jud come true, but so does her and Curly's death wish for him. In his role of predator and rival Jud is an undesirable element in the community. Curly has told him, "In this country, they's two things you c'n do if you're a man. Live out of doors is one. Live in a hole is the other" (*O* 71). Curly fits the image of the hearty outdoorsman, and in the songs "Oh, What a Beautiful Mornin'" and "The Surrey with the Fringe on Top" he is identified with nature and with such simple and innocent pleasures as a horse-and-buggy ride. Jud, however, fits the image of the reclusive cave-dweller. He hides indoors, pursues a dark obsession with pornography, and in the song "Lonely Room" is portrayed as an antisocial outsider.

Knowing that Jud will not heed his advice to "do sumpin healthy onct in a while" and thus perhaps earn his place in the community, Curly, somewhat shockingly, encourages him to commit suicide (*O* 71). Laurey, eager to free herself of Jud's relentless sexual pursuit, makes a similarly brutal statement by telling him, "somebody orta shoot you" (*O* 118). In a darkly humorous manner Hammerstein's libretto further emphasizes the community's desire to see Jud gone. Curly's grotesquely funny song "Poor Jud Is Daid" makes death attractive to Jud by claiming people would mourn his passing and reveal their previously hidden affection for him at his funeral. Ironically, nobody onstage actually feels sorry for Jud when he does die.

As good Americans, however, the characters in both versions of the play want to see justice served regarding Jud's death. While it is reported that Jud fell on his knife in his struggle with Curly, there is no clear evidence that Jud is responsible for his own death, and the town elders recommend that Curly submit himself to a hearing to establish his innocence or guilt in the matter. In *Green Grow the Lilacs* the community takes the incident very seriously, and Curly spends three days in jail awaiting his trial. Although the play ends on the encouraging note that Curly and Laurey get to spend their delayed wedding night together before Curly's hearing, it is unclear as the curtain falls whether Curly will go free.

Hammerstein treats this problematic episode rather lightheartedly. In *Oklahoma!* justice is done much more swiftly, and there is no ambiguity concerning Curly's fate. Instead of being thrown in jail, Curly is given a trial on the spot and set free within a mere "twenty minutes" so that he and Laurey can embark on their honeymoon and begin their new life together (*O* 142). Furthermore, Hammerstein added a humorous touch to Curly's trial by having the community member who serves as the judge coach him to answer the court's questions in such a way that he not implicate himself in Jud's death. "The plea is self-defense," the judge shouts even before Curly can finish describing the fight, and this interpretation is echoed by an enthusiastic crowd of witnesses (*O* 144). The libretto for *Oklahoma!* thus leaves no doubt that the townspeople are happy to rule Jud's death a suicide. With Jud's disappearance the community has been purged of a sick element, and life can go on peacefully. Theresa Helburn called Curly's trial "a triumph of American justice," and what this triumph demonstrates is that Americans, while eager to embrace good-natured and industrious foreigners like the peddler, are unafraid to act against their enemies, in their midst or abroad.[18] Ironically, although the trial scene ends the play on a note of optimism, Hammerstein's nonchalant treatment of Jud's death eerily evokes the disregard for human life during times of war.

In transforming a Depression-era tale of America's pioneer days into a wartime celebration of optimism and patriotism, the Theatre Guild not only redefined musical theatre but redefined an entire swath of America. The production of *Oklahoma!* converted the American prairie into a heartland: the cowboys and farmers of the musical were the very boys being asked to go to war, and the play, rather than mocking them as rubes, praises their character and values. Although *Oklahoma!* raised eyebrows while it was being created, it soon emerged as a major source of optimism about America's future, invigorating Americans in the face of World War II and defining the nation in a way that is still felt today.

Oklahoma! played on Broadway uninterrupted until 1948 and toured the country for a decade. All over the United States, people were hearing the show's tuneful songs on the radio and listening to a phenomenon that the Theatre Guild had invented—an original cast recording featuring most of the musical's songs accompanied by a complete orchestra. During the run of *Oklahoma!* the Guild also went to special lengths to associate the production with the war effort. When Alfred Drake was called up for military duty, Lawrence Langner made a special plea to the draft board that Drake's performance as Curly constituted a contribution to the American cause; Drake was allowed to stay and play his part. *Oklahoma!* was one of a few Broadway shows that featured special matinees that allowed patrons to purchase a war bond in lieu of buying a ticket. At each performance of the sold-out show, any returned tickets were reserved for soldiers on leave in New York, and the Theatre Guild created a touring production of the musical for the USO.[19]

Oklahoma! "was a success," Agnes de Mille remembered,

> because of the time in which it appeared. . . . We were well into the war and we were beginning to face up to the fact that it was going to be a long, costly and tragic war. Hitler held all of Europe; Japan held all of the Pacific. New York City was a great staging area, and for the next two years there were to be a double row of uniformed men standing at the back for every performance and watching this jolly, light-hearted show with tears streaming down their cheeks. Because what they were going overseas to die for was what this show was about: fresh air, turned earth, hardiness, friendship, trust.[20]

With Rodgers and Hammerstein's touch, the audience's view of the state of Oklahoma—less than a decade ago the locale of droughts and sandstorms and a place from which people fled in desperate need to survive—was changed into the image of a wholesome heartland, the backbone of American identity. "I think we succeeded in putting Oklahoma on the map," Theresa Helburn wrote to Philip Barry shortly after the musical had opened. "We hope that ultimately we will have completely destroyed its aroma of dust bowls and Okies because this is really the loveliest show you ever saw."[21]

The lasting effect of the Theatre Guild's efforts can be seen to this day. While producing a boisterously optimistic show in order to rally Americans was nothing new (although it is associated more with wartime Hollywood than with the theatre), the Guild went beyond simple patriotism. The producers of *Oklahoma!* were not merely playing to the masses and taking advantage of the economic opportunity provided by the wartime theatre market: *Oklahoma!* as imagined was, for its day, a daring aesthetic gamble, and its creators redefined a part of the nation along with the structure of the American musical on their way to commercial and critical success.

Notes

1. Theresa Helburn, "Story of *Oklahoma!*" in *Oklahoma!* souvenir program, Theatre Guild Collection, Yale Collection of American Literature, Beinecke Rare Book and Manuscript Library, Yale University (hereafter cited as YCAL).

2. Some scholars argue that Jerome Kern and Oscar Hammerstein's *Show Boat* (1927) was the first integrated musical.

3. In addition to producing *Porgy and Bess* the Theatre Guild had previously staged several editions of the revue *The Garrick Gaieties* in 1925, 1926, and 1930, a musical adaptation of Molière's *The School for Husbands* in 1933, and the revue *Parade* in 1935.

4. *A Wayward Quest: The Autobiography of Theresa Helburn* (Boston: Little, Brown, 1960), 285, 282.

5. This was something that could not be said of the traditional folksongs Riggs had originally included in his play. A contemporary reviewer had noted that Riggs's audiences "complained of the native songs as interruptions rather than atmosphere" ("New York Agrees," On Boston Boards, *Boston Transcript*, Feb. 2, 1931).

6. Agnes de Mille to Theresa Helburn, Sep. 24, 1942, Theatre Guild Correspondence, YCAL.

7. Lawrence Langner, "Article on Rouben Mamoulian for Lupton A. Wilkinson," Oct. 30, 1946, Theatre Guild Correspondence, YCAL.

8. Helburn, *Wayward Quest*, 284.

9. Theresa Helburn, "Inside *Oklahoma!*" Theatre Guild Correspondence, YCAL; Helburn, "Story of *Oklahoma!*"; Max Wilk, *OK: The Story of Oklahoma!* (New York: Applause, 2002), 171.

10. Helburn, "Inside *Oklahoma!*"

11. Oscar Hammerstein, *Oklahoma!* (New York: Random House, 1943), 34. Subsequent references will be cited parenthetically in the text.

12. Agnes de Mille, "Scenario for Ballet in *Oklahoma!*" Agnes de Mille Papers, Sophia Smith Collection, Smith College.

13. Agnes de Mille, interview by Sylvia Fine Kaye, transcript of the television program "Musical Comedy Tonight," Jan. 30, 1979, Agnes de Mille Collection, Jerome Robbins Dance Collection, New York Public Library for the Performing Arts.

14. Lynn Riggs, *Green Grow the Lilacs* promptbook, Theatre Guild Collection, YCAL, scene 4, p. 20. Lynn Riggs, *Green Grow the Lilacs* (New York: Samuel French, 1930), 44–45; subsequent references to the French edition will be cited parenthetically in the text.

15. I am grateful to Harriet Alonso for pointing out the parallel between Ado Annie and women in post–World War II America.

16. Helburn, "Inside *Oklahoma!*"

17. See also Leo Gaffney, "Illusion Sacrificed to Reality in New TG Play," *Boston Advertiser*, Dec. 14, 1930.

18. Helburn, "Inside *Oklahoma!*"

19. Lawrence Langner to Local Board No. 20, Nov. 2, 1943, Theatre Guild Correspondence, YCAL; *New York Times*, "Shows for Bonds," Oct. 3, 1944; Lynn Farnol, "Celebrating the Tenth Anniversary of Rodgers and Hammerstein," Theatre Guild Correspondence, YCAL, 8.

20. Agnes de Mille, "Final Remarks in the Tribute to Rodgers at the Benefit for the Museum of the City of New York," Agnes de Mille Collection, Jerome Robbins Dance Collection, New York Public Library for the Performing Arts.

21. Theresa Helburn to Philip Barry, April 7, 1943, Theatre Guild Correspondence, YCAL.

Precious Time

An Alternative Reading of Thornton Wilder's *Our Town* and William Saroyan's *The Time of Your Life* as Pre–World War II Dramas

Anne Fletcher

AMERICAN DRAMA OF THE 1930s is often investigated in terms of its response to the Great Depression. Viewed in this light, the dramas selected for review here are polemic and potently political, as characterized by the quintessential American "agitprop" style of Clifford Odets and his poetic and psychologically realistic commentaries on the American sociopolitical scene. Studies highlight the dramas' depiction of the abject poverty experienced by America's citizenry and the nation's overall malaise; some trace the transition from agitprop to socialist realism as the international political scene switched to the Popular Front. Occasionally dramatic literature of the second half of the decade is considered as illustrative of turbulence abroad (*Idiot's Delight,* for example), but the years 1938 to 1941, the interstices between the Depression and World War II, have been by and large ignored. Historian Richard M. Ketchum calls these the "borrowed years."[1] In his book on this time prior to America's formal entry to the war, he draws on his personal experience as a teenager, going through the daily routine of a typical young man his age, mostly oblivious to his father's business struggles during the Depression and unaware of the rise of fascism abroad, until the attack on Pearl Harbor forced the American public to action. It is in these years that *Our Town* and *The Time of Your Life* were written and brought to the stage, and it was to this naive American public that they played. As the history of the theatre continually illustrates, the dramatic literati are often "ahead of the curve" in terms of politics and international relations; theatre practitioners are often activists. It is not surprising, then, that Thornton Wilder's and William Saroyan's plays are imbued with political savvy.

Albert Wertheim's recent book, *Staging the War*, focuses on plays in light of America's engagement in World War II. Wertheim briefly addresses *Our Town* and *The Time of Your Life* similarly and in close proximity to each other.[2] In *American Drama between the Wars* Jordan Miller and Winifred Frazer follow their discussion of *Our Town* with that of *The Time of Your Life*, but they dismiss Saroyan's work as simply "fantasy."[3] Other works allude to religion in Wilder's plays and an existential dilemma in Saroyan's, but no one fully scrutinizes the dramaturgy of these playwrights as it relates both on the macro level to the impending Second World War and on a micro level to personal examinations of metaphysics and philosophical practices.

American drama, at the close of the 1930s, like the country itself as it confronted military conflict, seemed to adopt any form and content that defended the United States against outside threats. Isolationism and pacifism turned to patriotism as Americans entered combat. Even at the mid-decade apex of political theatre activity, the American audience still adhered to common myths of Americana and still relied on the narrative of the "American Dream." These myths provided comfort as the war approached, but Wilder and Saroyan use "Americana" subversively, and their works contrast with the patently patriotic turns taken by such dramatists as Elmer Rice and Robert Sherwood. Wilder and Saroyan subtly question "American values" and the indigenous American hero of the "straight-shooter" variety or that of the rugged individual, implicitly offering alternatives to American notions of patriotism and life itself.

Both Wilder and Saroyan have been accused of romanticizing American life, of sentimentalizing, and of playing to their audience's collective nostalgia. Tom Scanlan, in *Family, Drama, and American Dreams*, rightfully asserts that the perpetual view of *Our Town* as "sweet" is a problem of receptivity, emanating from the audience's perpetual desire to reclaim a past that Wilder would say never really was.[4] The same can be said of *The Time of Your Life*, to which the accusation of "escapism" has been leveled. "Linked to this charge . . . was the fact that Saroyan was not fashionably political; he supported no 'ism' and was therefore accused of lacking a social conscience."[5] Both plays are sprinkled with wry humor and underlying ironies that combat sentimentality. Both playwrights question the normative American philosophies of hard work, self-reliance, independence, and even free enterprise. *Our Town* problematizes the insularity of Grover's Corners and presents the human instinct to rush thoughtlessly through our daily lives, culminating in the admonition that mindfulness, true presence, and the ability to "realize life" are crucial. *The Time of Your Life* focuses on the penance of its agent of action and, in a Chekhovian combination of tragic and comic elements, examines the relationship between life and work. An itinerant pinball player delivers a "set speech" on the American work ethic; a prostitute acts out her fantasy of achieving the "American Dream" of marrying a doctor; and a Kit Carson figure arrives on the scene.

Juxtaposing *Our Town* and *The Time of Your Life* and reading them in light of pre–World War II American political sentiments, I employ a unique vocabulary, drawing on phenomenology, Buddhist principles, and time theory to reexamine these American "classics" and their position as prewar dramas. I touch on how Saroyan calls into question national myths, undercutting tragedy with humor in the face of fascism. I argue that Wilder manipulates time, employing what time theorists call "tenselessness" in a manner that foreshadows the military conflict to come, or at least the inevitability of deaths, and that both playwrights' alleged sentimentalism promotes not escapism in the face of an impending war but practical philosophical strategies for audiences to employ in troubled times. Each of these playwrights advocates introspection, contemplation, and a personalized approach to life rather than simply a collective reaction to outside threats.

I have purposely selected Buddhism (rather than transcendentalism) and phenomenology as it is employed in performance studies (rather than the phenomenology of Heidegger or, later, Derrida). I have also elected to employ "new" time theory rather than Einstein's theory of relativity or Stephen Hawking's thoughts on the history of time and space-time. I choose the methodological tools of Buddhism, the performance studies brand of phenomenology, and new time theory because they can be effectively used as personal philosophical approaches to life in chaotic times. An examination of the plays through the contemporary lenses of phenomenology, Buddhism, and time theory not only points to their relevance today but extends critical discussion and offers a new lexicon to use in play analysis itself.

Our Town has been exhaustively explored in terms of its staging, often as it recalls Wilder's early one-acts in structure and theme, sometimes as it compares to Asian theatrical forms; Saroyan's work, especially since his first literary "huzzahs" were earned as a writer of short stories, is considered in light of his deployment of "kitchen-sink" (if poetic) realism, with his lengthy and specific stage directions. At face value, then, Wilder and Saroyan would not seem particularly good dramaturgical bedfellows. I find them much more philosophically compatible, however, than, at face value, they appear to be.

Wilder plays to the collective unconscious of his audience, offering Grover's Corners as a microcosm for the world; but at the same time, through Emily's realization that no person truly lives life, he suggests that, individually, we might consider a mindful approach to our existence and thus build to a collective "Oneness." Wilder's metaphysical and dramaturgical construct concerns the relationship of the individual to the ontological whole. His teleological study reflects the structural relationships of part to whole in natural as well as metaphysical schemata.

Saroyan explores the binary of hope versus despair, most evident in the character of Joe but also with regard to the misfits who inhabit the saloon. Saroyan's saloon is *his* microcosm, but in contrast to Wilder's it is peopled with the walking wounded, society's exceptions versus Wilder's depiction of society's "rules." Infused with some of the futility expressed by the later avant-garde writers Saroyan would champion, the play reflects the playwright's sense of "cosmic disorder" and "spiritual vacuity."[6] *The Time of Your Life* ultimately follows a structural pattern that expresses the notion of the comic spirit as integrative and regenerative. "For Saroyan, art is a way toward health, toward reconciliation."[7] In this way, although their means may differ, both Wilder and Saroyan strive for similar ends. Saroyan copes with life's disarray; conversely, Wilder, through repeated rituals, presents life's order.

The strategies I have deployed, variously and in combination, include reading the plays in the light of the "beingness" of phenomenology, with an eye to the practice of "mindfulness"; the concepts of "witnessing" and of "attachments," "desires," and "Oneness" from Buddhist thought; and from the discipline of time theory I draw on the vocabulary of time theorists using notions of "tensed" versus "tenseless" language. It is at the nexus of these areas of study, tempered with the more familiar tools of new historicism, that I find Wilder and Saroyan most simpatico. Reading the texts through these lenses emphasizes their pre–World War II messages and serves to bracket the playwrights' comments on what it means to be American.

Being in the World: The Phenomenology of *Our Town* and *The Time of Your Life*

As artists both Wilder and Saroyan contemplated the efficacy of their art and the notion of "being." Both address "beingness" through their characters in the worlds of their plays. Influenced by his friendship with Gertrude Stein, Wilder adopted the Neoplatonic idea of a "group mind" and "Oneness," borrowing from Dante for the last act of *Our Town*. He sought to express the eternal and the universal that exist in the collective human mind, and by abandoning realism he emphasized what he thought of as the "eternal present" of the stage itself. In his chapter on Wilder in William Demastes's *Realism and the American Dramatic Tradition,* Christopher Wheatley interprets this notion of the eternal present with regard to Wilder's nonrealistic staging techniques. Wheatley identifies the locus of the stage itself, and consequently the staging and viewing of a play, as always in the present tense and realism as anathema to the present (presence) Wilder sought.[8] Thornton Wilder posited that European determinism is reified by realism, which in turn is patriarchal, and, more important, in its positivism it exists only in the past tense. "The theatre, occurring in the present tense, should escape determinism and authority *by presenting being in action.*"[9] Wheatley asserts that the kind of truth to which Wilder aspired "cannot be expressed in purely realist terms, since *the mystery of faith* is an expression of the *possible,* not the *probable.*"[10] I extend Wheatley's notion of the historical moment and assertions regarding Wilder's expression of religious beliefs into the arena of Buddhist thoughts on time and space.

William Saroyan's overriding philosophy is typified by his statement that "[m]y work is writing, but my real work is *being.*"[11] It is fitting, then, for Saroyan to create in Joe a protagonist who does not work and who exists solely to "be," who in his "being" reveals more about life than characters who "do." In fact, Saroyan's stage directions at the opening of the play set Joe up "as though he were trying very hard to discover how to live."[12]

I emphasize the phenomenological in these playwrights because their characters experience the world vibrantly, describe it vividly, and draw important conclusions from their perceptions of being in the world. The fictional characters, unwittingly perhaps, practice the phenomenological research process within the context of a fictive world.

Of course, the most frequently quoted moment of *Our Town,* Emily's farewell speech ("Do human beings ever realize life while they live it— every, every minute?")[13] illustrates the play's message, but there are numerous other passages that support taking a phenomenological peek at the work. Emily enumerates the simple pleasures she must leave: "clocks ticking—and my butternut tree! . . . And Mama's sunflowers—and food and coffee—and new-ironed dresses and hot baths" (83)—all possible subjects for contemplation, sensory appreciation, and even meditation. The simple, honest, daily activities Wilder's characters execute (snapping peas, patting a horse, delivering the milk, sipping a soda) are all part and parcel of his underlying message that it is in living each day, each moment, fully that we may find peace. In *The Time of Your Life* Joe echoes precisely the same sentiments on more than one occasion, but he undercuts spiritual insights by attributing them to the consumption of alcohol. He implies that by remaining still and by executing selectivity in terms of which tasks to tackle, we might find serenity. For example, when asked why he drinks, he responds: "Because I don't like to be gypped. Because I don't like to be dead most of the time and just a little alive every once in a long time. If I don't drink, I become fascinated by unimportant things—like everybody else. I get busy. I do things. All kinds of stupid little things. Proud, selfish, *ordinary* things. . . . Now I don't do anything. *I live all the time*" (417). He continues: "Twenty-four hours. Out of the twenty-four hours at least twenty-three and a half are . . . dull, boring, empty, and murderous. Minutes on the clock, *not time of living*. It doesn't make any difference who you are or what you do. . . . That goes on for days . . . and weeks and months and years . . . and the first thing you know *all* the years are dead. All the minutes are dead. You yourself are dead" (418).

It seems that Wilder admonishes us to appreciate each moment and to acknowledge it no matter how mundane it may seem; Saroyan advises that we take a slightly but not significantly different path—that we be wary of allowing the banal to engulf us lest we forget to experience life as it passes.

Buddhist Thought and the Plays: Rehearsal and Performance

Phenomenology can be related to aspects of Buddhist thought. Whereas a phenomenological approach requires one to experience "beingness" and to describe this presence in the world nonjudgmentally, Buddhist thought requires that one go a step further and *practice*. Buddhist practice involves, through meditation, the goal of living with an appreciation of life in all its sweetness and sorrow, sans desires or attachments, and the acknowledgment of a universal "Oneness." *Vipassana* (insight) meditation is "a set of mental activities specifically aimed at experiencing a state of uninterrupted Mindfulness."[14] "Mindfulness," living fully in the present, is a cornerstone of Buddhist thought. The practice involves focusing one's attention, according to one method "single-pointedly" on an object, to others, focusing on the breath. "Mindfulness is non-judgmental observation."[15] Mindfulness is also characterized by an "awareness of change . . . the passing flow of experience. It is watching things as they are changing. It is seeing the birth, growth, and maturity of all phenomena. It is watching phenomena decay and die. Mindfulness is watching things moment by moment. . . . One just sits back and watches the show. . . . It is watching the thing arising and passing away. . . . In Mindfulness, one watches the universe within."[16]

Joe seems to agree with Buddhist practice when he says, "Living is an art. . . . It takes a lot of rehearsing for a man to get to be himself" (438). It might seem, then, that while Saroyan points to *rehearsing* life, Wilder's characters *perform* life.

In the practice of mindfulness, one is simultaneously a participant and an observer. This dual function is called "witnessing." The Stage Manager in *Our Town* admonishes Emily before she returns, "You not only live it; but you watch yourself living it" (75). As Rex Burbank places it in his book on Wilder, "From the vantage point of eternity . . . she observes the scene of her twelfth birthday—the full intensity of each moment, good or bad, through *the agency of consciousness, love.*"[17]

Another key element in the practice of meditation lies in the breath and an understanding that each inhalation and exhalation is, in essence, a "little" death. Buddhist practice focuses on the process of confronting death but not in a morbid way. One of the principal reasons for practicing meditation lies in the notion of "letting go," as we will in death, of both the mind and the body and the abandonment of our self-identification based on physical and psychological properties. Another factor is the detriment to our spiritual health of chronological time as we experience it. A Buddhist and a leading practitioner in the field of death and dying, Stephen Levine addresses specific practices in both *Who Dies?* and *A Year to Live,* an exercise in living one full year as if it were his last. In *The Power of Now: A Guide to Spiritual Enlightenment* theologian Eckhart Tolle advises:

> End the delusion of time. . . . To be identified with your mind is to be trapped in time: the compulsion to live almost exclusively through memory and anticipation. This creates an endless preoccupation with past and future and an unwillingness to honor and acknowledge the present moment and allow it to be. The compulsion arises because the past gives you an identity and the future holds the promise of salvation. . . . Both are illusions.[18]

A Buddhist saying admonishes, "While alive, live as a dead person, thoroughly dead"; and a Zen koan says, "Show me your Original face, the Face you had before your parents were born."[19] Neither expression is intended to confound the would-be Buddhist practitioner; each is meant to remind its recipient that time as we traditionally view it is irrelevant, that there is only oneness.

Buddhism acknowledges the oneness of everything. Those who practice the religion and not just the meditative practices, of course, respect all living things equally (termites and flies command as much respect as human beings). Reincarnation is part of the faith as well. Wilder and Saroyan express the concept of the universal "One" in various ways, and although neither exhibits a proclivity toward reincarnation, both evoke a sense of repetition. Saroyan's epigraph to *The Time of Your Life* succinctly sums it up. Here are but a few of the precepts it espouses: "In the time of your life—live"; "Place in matter and in flesh the least of values, for these are the things that hold death and must pass away"; and "Remember that every man is a variation of yourself" (385). The title of the play, of course, emphasizes Saroyan's concern with time and being, the phrase "The Time" alluding to being in the moment but the use of the word *time* simultaneously denoting its passage and mutability.

Although definitely Christian in origin and content, the cemetery scene in *Our Town,* where the Stage Manager muses that there is something eternal and that something has to do with humans, is akin to Buddhist thought in its acknowledgment of the "One." As Burbank puts it, "All the problems and joys, the grief and happiness, and the love and indifference, it is suggested, are dissolved in *the transcendent Whole* . . . the Mind of God."[20] In his description of Dudley, one of the "plainest of people,"[21] Saroyan acknowledges this Oneness: "His gestures are wild. His ego is disjointed and epileptic. And yet deeply he possesses the same wholeness of spirit, and directness of energy, that is in all species of animals" (Clurman 399).

Extending the manner in which Calonne interprets Saroyan's epigraph, we can infer other Buddhist tendencies on the part of the playwright, as we witness "the self exfoliating out into 'infinite delight and mystery.'"[22] This notion of exfoliating, or gradually removing layers, is a major tenet of Buddhist thought, as is the idea of expanding and dissolving into infinity. While enlightenment is possible within the confines of time and space as we think of them, at death we join the Oneness, according to Buddhism, in a series of encounters with the colors of the Bardos, the liminal spaces on the trajectory to the ultimate Oneness, described vividly in *The Tibetan Book of the Dead.* The closer our earthly practice approximates an expression of the One, the more quickly we will reach the true One. In Christian terms these concepts parallel the best practices of "doing unto others" in our earthly lives, living well as we move toward eternal salvation.

Calonne examines *The Time of Your Life* as it exhibits a tension between romanticism and existentialism, whereas I see the play as Buddhist balance in performance—as an extension of the serenity and delicate balance the Buddhist practitioner seeks in all aspects of life. I concur with Calonne's conclusion that Saroyan can play these oppositional philosophies off each other because, at heart, they are interrelated.

The name Saroyan gives the winning horse on which Joe bets, "Precious Time," is another of the playwright's subtle nods to the principles of Buddhism. Time in the prewar years was indeed precious, to be savored, as is all the time of our lives, and Joe's horse wins. The horse in the play is a "long shot," and when Nick, more of a betting man, asks Joe how he knew on which horse to place his bet, Joe "roars" his answer, "Faith, faith" (409).

Saroyan's boldest "Buddhist" statement is manifested in the presence of the mysterious character of the Arab and in Joe's translation of the Arab's trope, "No foundation. All the way down the line. What. What-not. Nothing. I go walk and look at the sky" (425). In the following few lines Joe encapsulates Buddhist thought, but once again he undercuts his philosophical statement through his insistence that the metaphysicality he describes is possible only through the use of alcohol:

> What? What-not? That means this side, that side. Inhale, exhale. What: birth. What-not: death. The inevitable, the astounding, the magnificent seed of growth and decay in all things. Beginning, and end. That man, in his own way, is a prophet. He is one who, with the help of *beer* is able to reach that state of deep understanding in which what and what-not, the reasonable and the unreasonable, are *one*. (425)

Both Saroyan and Wilder intertwine their ontological expressions with their statements on war and on the American character. It is this fascinating juxtaposition of notions of the eternal and the ephemeral that strengthen the plays' relationships to World War II.

In *Our Town* Joe Crowell is identified with the Second World War in the Stage Manager's comment, "What business he had picking a quarrel with the Germans we can't make out to this day, but it all seemed perfectly clear to us at the time" (7). Here, too, the Stage Manager alludes to the talents lost in the waging of war when he mentions that Joe would have made a fine engineer had he lived. While Wilder seldom specifically references the impending war in *Our Town,* he subtly characterizes war in general. The play is not necessarily pacifist but rather incorporates war into the schematic of life and its cycle, as illustrated by the replacement of Joe Crowell with his younger brother later, perhaps a pragmatic Americanization of the notion of reincarnation.

In his enumeration of the material objects that will go into the cornerstone, the Stage Manager foregrounds Wilder's emphasis on daily life and culture, musing that it is more important than the Treaty at Versailles. And when he describes the Civil War gravestones, he alludes to misguided patriotism and the overall lack of understanding the average person has with regard to issues of war. "All they knew was the name, friends—the United States of America. The United States of America. And they went and died about it" (67). Wertheim sees Dr. Gibb's fascination with the Civil War, and Mr. Webb's with Napoleon, as an implication that one day, in the not-so-distant future, monuments from the impending conflict would become a list of tourist attractions, trivialized and commodified just as the Civil War battlegrounds were by 1938.[23]

Saroyan creates a direct correlation between the action of his play and the war already raging in Europe. News of the conflict enters the world of the saloon on several occasions, although the characters often reject it. Whenever the newsboy enters, as an act of charity Joe purchases every copy of the paper. He then glances at the headlines and discards the papers, which in turn are taken up by the Arab, who reads the headlines and utters his postmodern refrain, "No foundation. All the way down the line." A striking relationship between the fictive world of *The Time of Your Life* and the "real" world can be constructed by taking a cursory look at *New York Times* headlines at the time of the play's opening. Synchronistically, an excerpt from a front-page story on October 25, 1939, the day of the play's premiere reads: "Hitler and his Nazi gang pretend to sympathize with the Arabs and to care for them. But to them, Arabs are cheap and have been downgraded to rank 13 among human beings in a classification system invented by the criminal Nazi mind, and Jews were placed right below that rank as Number 14."

Near the play's end Joe sends Tom out to purchase magazines and a map of Europe. The magazine titles encapsulate the play's messages— *Life, Liberty,* and *Time!* And the vaudevillian character, Harry, works reading the newspaper into his act: "I go out and buy a morning paper. What the hell do I want with a morning paper? . . . I go out and buy a morning paper. Thursday, the twelfth. Maybe the headline's about me. I take a quick look. No. The headline is not about me. It's about Hitler. Seven thousand miles away. I'm here. Who the hell is Hitler?" (428). Harry epitomizes the American general public of the borrowed years (1938–41), as most people focused on their personal lives and livelihoods, blissfully unaware of, or in denial about, dangerous machinations abroad and the effect they would soon have on American life as they knew it.

Harry alludes to the war two more times in his monologues: "A fat guy bumps his stomach into an old lady . . . Boom. I don't know. It may mean war. War. Germany. England. Russia. WAAAAAR"; and,

"I'm standing there. I didn't do anything to anybody. Why should I be a soldier? BOOOOOOOOOM! *WAR!* War. *I* retreat. *I* hate war. I move to Sacramento" (401–2).

Vaudeville, of course, presents a uniquely American forum of expression, and the irony of the seriousness of the subject matter within the framework of the popular entertainment idiom strengthens Saroyan's message. That the conflict of war could be expressed through the action of a corpulent man crashing into a fat lady is ingenious indeed! Once again, we must remember, this action is set in 1939, not after the events of December 7, 1941.

Elsie, the woman Dudley loves, speaks of the results of the war from firsthand experience. Then she projects the unpleasant future possibilities: "Every night I watch over poor, dying men. I hear them breathing, crying, talking in their sleep"; and, "The time for the new pathetic war has come. Let's hurry before they dress you, stand you in line, hand you a gun, and have you kill and be killed" (449). Elsie's comments are couched in realistic terms, and she brings the war closer to the reader/audience, all the more so because of San Francisco's position as home of a military base.

Two other aspects of *The Time of Your Life* as they relate to America's relationship to the war deserve note here. First, Saroyan draws the character of Blick to recall the image of Hitler, describing the character in his stage directions as entering "with the manner of a petty fascist tyrant" and as having a demeanor "unmistakably that of the Gestapo" (22). Second, Joe has remained safely isolated from the world for three years. He explains that he has spent this time trying to live a life that does not do harm to others, in essence a pacifist's life. At the play's conclusion, Joe leaves the saloon, Saroyan's commentary on America's foreign policies. As Calonne points out, Joe's physical departure from the saloon, symbolic of his abandonment of isolationism, occurred (at the time of the play's premier) just one month after Germany's invasion of Poland.[24]

Precious Time, Borrowed Time: Time Theory and the Plays

Like phenomenology (thinking about what it means to be in the world), "time theory," or contemplation of the notions of past, present, and future, is undoubtedly as old as humankind itself. Philosophical discourse is marked by seminal figures' explanations of the passage and meaning of time; and although vocabulary changes across generations, two pronounced approaches to time theory emerge: "presentism" and "eternalism," or "actualism"—frequently referred to in the field as "A-

Theory" and "B-Theory." Presentists believe that neither the future nor the past exists; eternalists purport that past and future people, places, and events do exist. A-Theory, or the A-Series, or those who espouse A-Properties are represented by the presentists who consider time through the employment of definite verb tenses (*was, is, will,* etc.), constituting "tensed theory." The A-Properties to which presentists refer are those of "presentness," "pastness," and "futurity." These theorists consider tense to be "an objective feature of reality."[25]

For the presentist the "'present' is not one whose temporal existence varies according to context."[26] B-Theory, or the B-Series (B-Properties), believes that all successively ordered events have the same ontological status; these theorists propose that all there is to be said about the world can be said "once and for all." The temporal relationships the B-Theorists employ are expressed in broad strokes—"earlier than," "later than," and "simultaneous with."[27] The most salient issues in applying new time theory to *Our Town* and *The Time of Your Life* relate to the concepts of linearity (or succession) and nonlinearity, the present, and simultaneity. This is not to say that Thornton Wilder and William Saroyan deliberately deployed specific time theories in their works but rather to note that notions of time theory pervaded the prewar years every bit as much as they do today, and the playwrights could not help but have been affected by the zeitgeist. Surely neither Wilder nor Saroyan escaped the impact of Einstein's theory of relativity, published more than a decade and a half before *Our Town* and *The Time of Your Life*.

Thornton Wilder spent a lifetime toying with time in his narrative structures. As an aficionado of James Joyce he so revered *Finnegan's Wake* that one critic leveled a plagiarism charge, asserting that in his creation of *Our Town* Wilder had taken directly from the novel.[28] Wilder's earlier one-act plays, such as *Pullman Car Hiawatha, The Happy Journey to Trenton and Camden,* and *The Long Christmas Dinner* all toy with time. *Pullman Car Hiawatha* has been said to combine "all levels of time and space . . . relating the life of the mind to the life of the universe."[29] As early as 1931, in *The Long Christmas Dinner,* Wilder utilized time and space to underscore the inevitable world war. In this play the character Charles states, "Time certainly goes very fast in a great new country like this [America]," to which Cousin Ermengarde responds, "Well, time must be passing very slowly in Europe with this dreadful war going on."[30]

Time theorists acknowledge that time and space are inextricably linked and that concepts of time cannot be expressed without reference to notions of space. Wilder's thoughts on playwriting and his expressions of time and space in his plays point to his concept of metaphysics—the

idea that by being human we relate to natural phenomena, that beyond
the natural world lies "something eternal," a higher presence, and un-
derscoring the sense of eternity or Oneness is the feeling that reality
transcends time. By setting his plays in the perpetual present, consciously and for placement purposes alluding to geology and geography,
and by addressing a group mind, Wilder creates "on stage a present that
encompasses all time . . . an 'Act in Eternity.'"[31] Commenting retro-
spectively on the play, Wilder said, "My experience with *Our Town* con-
vinces me that the notion of time as immutable and consecutive action
is not the only one. In *Our Town* time was scrambled, liberated."[32]
Wilder's use of time in *Our Town* illustrates the playwright's search "for
a new form in which there will be perpetual counterpoint between the
detailed episode of daily life—the meal, the chat, the courtship and the
funeral—the ever present references to geological time and a distant
future for the millions of people who have repeated these moments."[33]

Wilder's belief that he was addressing the "group mind" of his audience and that his play's action took place in the "perpetual present"[34]
parallels notions of time as expressed both in Eastern philosophies and
by the tenseless theorists. As Burbank explains, "the quotidian scenes
(growing up, love and marriage, and death)" are seen "from different
perspectives of time and space and different metaphysical vantage points"
as the worldview of the play gradually expands to the "Mind of God."[35]
Wilder's Stage Manager presents the eternal by negation—he tells his
audience what is *not* eternal, thus employing a contrast between absence
and presence akin to Saroyan's "what" and "what-not."

Wilder's use of verbs supports tenseless time theory. Wheatley describes the play as "a series of gerunds, 'growing,' 'living,' 'marrying,'
'dying,' becoming nouns through enactment. The residents of Grover's
Corners are not identified by a past . . . but by their actions in the stage's
eternal present."[36] In fact, Wilder varies his verb tenses within a single
speech when the Stage Manager declares that the "First automobile's *goin'*
to come along in about five years—*belonged* to Banker Cartwright . . .
Lives up in the big house . . . " (2; my emphasis). Wilder signified the
specific years of the play's action (1901, 1904, 1913), but he conflates
time once again by having the Stage Manager name the participants in
the present production. The idea that names and dates of the company
performing the play be uttered aloud extends Wilder's notion of time
into another eternal present, that of every subsequent reader or audience
member from January 1938 to the calendar present. Viewed this way,
Our Town exists eternally, in 1901, 1904, 1913, 1938 (the year of its premiere), 2005, and beyond, promoting Wilder's attempt at constructing
what he called those "ever-present references."[37] Wilder's repeated use

of the words *thousands* and *millions* and his sensitive placement of geological references underscore his sense of both immediacy and eternity.
The First Dead Man in the cemetery comments, "And my Joel, who
knew the stars—he used to say it took millions of years for that little
speck o' light to git down to earth. . . . [T]hat's what he used to say—
millions of years" (85). Set against millions of years, one life is indeed
short and needs to be led not, as Simon Stimson says, "in a cloud of
ignorance . . . at the mercy of one self-centered passion, or another" but
with acuity (84). The Stage Manager operates in a sort of universal
time, referencing past, present, and future. We receive more backstory
at the wedding ceremony: we learn that Doc Gibbs died in 1930, and,
of course, there is the simultaneity of time in Emily's return; whereas
the Stage Manager is in present time, Emily is in the past but at the
age of her death, and the other participants relive or reenact the past
in the moment of the present.

Although William Saroyan plays less with linearity than Wilder does,
couching his play's action within a causal framework, he expands the
notion of time by including the Kit Carson character and ending the
piece with Carson's statement about killing Blick: "I shot a man once.
In San Francisco. In 1939, I think it was. In October."[38] Calonne addresses Saroyan's expression of time as it relates to "his vision of the
self" and "the struggle for true being."[39] I see Saroyan's extension of
time as pervasively mythological and universal—observable not just by
his inclusion of Kit Carson and Carson's use of verb tense in his closing
statement but evident in the repeated ritual of the pinball player, in
Kitty's desire to live the American dream, in the vaudevillian's monologues, and the manner in which Joe, like absurdist or existential protagonists, passes his days in inactivity or perhaps Godot-like waiting.
Saroyan carefully places the play's action in time, 1939, by utilizing "The
Missouri Waltz" as the song Joe plays incessantly on the phonograph.
Popularized in the 1939 movie *The Story of Vernon and Irene Castle*,
starring Fred Astaire and Ginger Rogers, the song operates on one level
as a marker of time. Curiously, though, Saroyan's choice would reverberate in subsequent readings and productions of *The Time of Your Life*,
as "The Missouri Waltz" later became synonymous with Harry Truman.

Temperament and Time: America Goes to War and Beyond

Both Wilder and Saroyan comment on the American temperament.
Wilder's thoughts on indigenous American drama and the manner of
presenting it in the eternal present stem from his view of Americans as
having "no stabilizing relation to any one place, nor to any community,

nor to any one moment in time."[40] Wilder sees Americans as "discon-nected,"[41] and Wheatley extends this idea to describe Americans as "rootless and oriented toward the present and the future," as having "an identity only *in action*"[42] (my emphasis). Surely William Saroyan would agree. Taken together, Wilder and Saroyan seem to assess the American spirit of the "borrowed years" as akin to the Greek notion of restlessness and expansion known as *polypragmasusae*. Whereas Wil-der's piece may be viewed as a cautionary tale, urging Americans to slow down and take time to "smell the roses," Saroyan creates a more active critique of the American way. The character of the Drunk is de-scribed by the playwright as a "champion of the Bill of Rights," and it is he who spouts off, "This is a free country, ain't it?" (388). Another stage direction indicates a "deep American naïveté and faith in the be-havior of each character."[43] When Harry, the would-be performer, asks McCarthy if his act is any good, McCarthy replies, "It's awful, but it's honest and ambitious, like everything else in this great country. . . . A most satisfying demonstration of the present state of the American body and soul" (427).

The saloon's pinball machine is the most ingenious of Saroyan's com-ments on Americana, more so even than the mythic Kit Carson's func-tion as the murderer of Blick. For this icon of laziness and of chance virtually explodes with American flags and music when someone hits the jackpot. Near the close of the play, the song "America" plays and the people in the saloon rise to their feet.

The coexistence of the contemplative, the compassionate, the comic, and the sublime in these two plays, with the turbulence and impending destruction of World War II, reflects the two extremes of American foreign policy—isolation/pacifism versus military involvement. Viewing the plays from the perspectives of phenomenology, Buddhism, and time theory enhances both their specificity with regard to the historical mo-ment and their universality. Phenomenologically speaking, we read or view the plays from our own places of being, receiving them in our individual contexts and appreciating them from our unique position-ality. By applying Buddhist thought we can delight in their expressions of the moment, drawing from Wilder and Saroyan practical tips for liv-ing peacefully. Whether we practice Buddhism or not, we can contem-plate relishing the moment and take from the plays the inherent joie de vivre they express. Finally, reading the plays through the lens of tenseless time theory, we can feel the eternal reverberations of *Our Town* and *The Time of Your Life*. Grover's Corners becomes anytime, any place: the conflict in Europe becomes any war, and we can contemplate the never-ending rituals of love, marriage, birth, death, and human conflict as they repeat themselves, eternally.

Notes

1. Richard M. Ketchum, *The Borrowed Years: 1938–1941—America on the Way to War* (New York: Doubleday, 1991), preface and 5–52.

2. See Albert Wertheim, *Staging the War: American Drama and World War II* (Bloomington: Indiana University Press, 2004), 19–21.

3. Jordan Y. Miller and Winifred L. Frazer, *American Drama between the Wars: A Critical History* (Boston: Twayne, 1997), 237–45.

4. Tom Scanlan, *Family, Drama, and American Dreams* (Westport, CT: Greenwood Press, 1978), 202.

5. David Stephen Calonne, *William Saroyan: My Real Work Is Being* (Chapel Hill: University of North Carolina Press, 1983), 3–4; Saroyan refused to claim his Pulitzer Prize for the play because he believed the award supported the capitalist philosophy with which he so fervently disagreed. That was his sociopolitical stance.

6. Ibid., 6.

7. Ibid., 7.

8. Christopher Wheatley, "Thornton Wilder, the Real, and Theatrical Realism," in *Realism and the American Dramatic Tradition,* ed. William B. Demastes (Tuscaloosa: University of Alabama Press, 1996), 144.

9. Ibid., 148–49 (my emphasis).

10. Ibid., 141 (my emphasis).

11. Cited in Calonne, *William Saroyan,* 8.

12. William Saroyan, *The Time of Your Life,* repr. in *Famous American Plays of the 1930s,* ed. Harold Clurman (New York: Dell, 1964), 387. Subsequent references to *The Time of Your Life* are from this edition and will be cited parenthetically in the text.

13. Thornton Wilder, *Our Town: A Play in Three Acts* (1938; repr., New York: Coward-McCann, with Samuel French, 1965), 83. Subsequent references are from the reprint edition and will be cited parenthetically in the text.

14. H. Gunaratana Mahathera, *Mindfulness in Plain English,* chap. 13, "Mindfulness (Sati)," http://www.saigon.com/~anson/ebud/mfneng/mind13.htm (accessed Nov. 7, 2005).

15. Ibid.

16. Ibid.

17. Rex Burbank, *Thornton Wilder* (New York: Twayne, 1961), 94 (my emphasis).

18. Eckhart Tolle, *The Power of Now: A Guide to Spiritual Enlightenment* (Novato, CA: New World Library, 1999), 40.

19. Ken Wilber, *The Essential Ken Wilber* (Boston: Shambhala, 1998), 172.

20. Burbank, *Thornton Wilder,* 95 (my emphasis).

21. Saroyan as cited in Calonne, *William Saroyan*, 90.

22. Ibid., 85.

23. Wertheim, *Staging the War*, 19–20.

24. Calonne, *William Saroyan*, 22.

25. William Lane Craig, "Adams on Actualism and Presentism," http://leaderu.com/offices/billcraig/docs/adamson.html (accessed Nov. 7, 2005). Craig is one of the main participants in the philosophical discourse concerning presentism.

26. Neil McKinnon, "Presentism and Consciousness," http://www.geocities.com/trolleylauncher/AJPPresentismConsciousnessFinal Version.htm (accessed Nov. 7, 2005).

27. Robert S. Brunbaugh, *Unreality and Time* (Albany: State University of New York Press, 1984), 2.

28. Jackson R. Bryer, *Conversations with Thornton Wilder* (Jackson: University Press of Mississippi, 1992), 42.

29. Burbank, *Thornton Wilder*, 71.

30. Thornton Wilder, *The Long Christmas Dinner* as cited in Burbank, *Thornton Wilder*, 151.

31. Burbank, *Thornton Wilder*, 89.

32. Bryer, *Conversations with Thornton Wilder*, 33.

33. Ibid.

34. Burbank, *Thornton Wilder*, 84–86.

35. Ibid., 90.

36. Wheatley, "Thornton Wilder," 151.

37. Bryer, *Conversations with Thornton Wilder*, 33.

38. Saroyan, *The Time of Your Life*, 480.

39. Calonne, *William Saroyan*, 87.

40. Wilder as quoted in Wheatley, "Thornton Wilder," 148–49.

41. Ibid.

42. Ibid., 150.

43. Saroyan, quoted in Clurman, *Famous American Plays*, 410.

Military Minstrelsy in
Text and Performance

kb saine

I N 1941 EXECUTIVE ORDER 8802 prompted a national evaluation
of the role and representation of blacks in the U.S. military. In
addition to "prohibiting discrimination in federal government and defense industry employment," the order also led to the assertion that the
number of blacks enlisted in the service should be directly proportional
to the nation's black population.

All branches of the military were deficient in their numbers and per-
centages of blacks enlisted. This was not due to a lack of interest or
intent within the black community: "The notion that blacks would gain
from the war, not as a gift of white goodwill but because the nation
needed the loyalty and manpower of African Americans, had been
sounded in every one of America's previous armed conflicts, and it continued to reverberate during World War II."[1] Due in large part to the
military's required literacy standards, however, and to physical differences between blacks and whites, recruiters routinely turned down those
blacks who volunteered (or who were later drafted) for service. With
the legislative push to increase black numbers, military personnel turned
to enlist northern blacks, who were afforded better educational opportunities than were southern blacks and could better meet the military's
standards. These newly enlisted northern blacks, accustomed to a common set of civil liberties and unaccustomed to strict laws of segregation,
moved into training camps predominantly located in the Jim Crow
South and run by white southerners. Essentially, as Daniel Kryder asserts in *Divided Arsenal*, the "War Department posted black troops to
areas where custom, law, and the police combined to severely constrain
their rights and actions."[2] Obvious racial tensions resulted. Government

leaders, whom Roosevelt appointed for the specific task of receiving complaints from both black soldiers and white military leaders and police, fielded numerous reports, but despite continuous collection of intelligence and onsite investigations, little advancement was directly made. The truth of the situation was that although the army's antidiscrimination policies were falling into place, its camps were so spread out, and so independent of one another, that the new laws proved impossible to enforce on a national level.

The results of investigations dealing with race-related conflicts and riots in military camps were often ignored by the War Department in favor of a retreat to "older formulas, . . . ascribing the difficulties to the stationing of northern African-Americans in the South and to the 'average Negro soldier's meager education, superstition, imagination, and excitability' which, coupled with regimentation, made him 'easily misled' and developed a 'mass state of mind.'"[3] Continuation of such sweeping excuses only enforced southern black soldiers' growing concerns that their voices would not be heard either by southern officials or the War Department, who held like opinions where race was concerned. The "War Department was known as the most discriminatory mainline federal agency, due in large part to its reputed domination by white southern personnel."[4] From 1941 to 1943 dissatisfaction and race-related violence continued to rise in the southern camps. The need for a set of actions to ameliorate tensions became obvious, both to boost troop morale and to maintain a sense of order.

The majority of the segregated black camps offered few prospects for entertainment and leisure activities. One of the War Department's major steps toward improving race relations and opportunities came in the form of a 1943 decree calling for the desegregation of all army camp facilities. In some camps this proved no issue, since the major confrontations documented were between black soldiers and white military police; most camps had few issues with black and white soldiers, who recognized their common goal. Many camps took small steps toward this end, enabling only black officers to enter into what would become common areas. In other camps segregation remained, either by choice of both parties or because the white, southern military police subversively maintained the old rules. Corporal William D. Lee, a black soldier stationed at Camp Adair, wrote in to the *Pittsburgh Courier* in July of 1943 to complain that there were "no places for us to have any fun at all. No Day Rooms no U.S.O. Clubs, no Service Clubs, and no Entertainment What So Ever [*sic*]."[5]

With no way to effectively enforce the new policies of integration, and with the majority of troops left with inadequate and substandard

facilities, the government, military leaders, and the black press continued to field desperate complaints and concerns from the soldiers. The
War Department responded with a series of initiatives and publications
intended to placate the discouraged and disgusted soldiers. With the
War Department "facing very low morale in black units," Kryder states,
"a typical recommended corrective program might include . . . patriotic
plays." One of the most prominent efforts of the War Department in
1943 was a "set of ameliorative techniques [involving] the equalization
of facilities and programs, primarily recreational ones, such as the construction of United Service Organizations (USO) facilities, and visits
to Southern camps by black entertainers and athletes."[6]

It was in this type of restorative action that the War Department
recognized the power of performance as a tool with which to entertain
and encourage the troops within a framework of equality. In newly integrated or newly established facilities soldiers of both races could enjoy
a potentially mutual and entertaining evening with very little interaction
(and therefore very little potential for conflict).

The *Pittsburgh Courier* carried many reviews of successful USO productions featuring predominant black performers. A performance at
Camp Jackson of the "Blue Ribbon Salute" featured "Earl Hines and
his band furnishing rocking rhythm and Billy Eckstein winning raves
with his romantic voice." Bill Bailey, Vivian Hines, Louis Jordan, and
"the kings of buffoonery, Patterson and Jackson," also added their performances to the review. The *Courier*'s claim that the Salute "received
double-barreled responses from our boys in service and civilians of both
races" indicates that this was one of the earlier, integrated opportunities
for the military to boost its troops' morale.[7]

In addition to these USO touring shows the War Department encouraged in-camp performances. It is not the intent of this essay to
assert that the War Department's encouragement of in-camp endeavors
was driven solely by a desire to discourage racial unrest but to acknowledge the War Department's recognition of the power of theatrical performance for use in rebuilding black trust and support.

The First World War proved the benefits of stage entertainment for
the troops in both amateur and professional venues. In the Second
World War the Special Service Division of the War Department established the framework for the production of the Soldier Shows to continue theatre's successful streak as encouragement for the troops. "In
most service commands, the Director, Special Services Division, War
Department, . . . placed one or more Theatrical Advisors for theatrical
activities." In June of 1942 the authority was granted through a War
Department circular for the special services officer to appoint "one or

more soldiers on full-time duty to assist the Soldier Shows production."
Instructions for the organizing of program personnel follow, with complete detail for the positions of program director, music director, technical director, drama director, publicity director, and radio director; playwrights, actors, and technical staff were to be chosen from among the camps' volunteers. The War Department essentially established, complete with a ranking order, absolute production staffs whose sole purpose in the military was the creation of the camps' shows.[8]

The War Department insisted that the greatest value of the Soldier Show performances was in their productions overseas, but the *Soldier Shows Guide* cites the advantage of soldiers working together on the productions in their own country before going overseas. Semantically, all directions are given in the present tense for productions "here at home," with the intent that when units reach isolated bases or theatres of operation, they will be prepared to produce entertainment anywhere. Fundamentally, while other soldiers were in antiartillery training, these War Department appointees engaged in theatre production training.

Unlike the touring USO shows, these performances can be best compared to Luther Billis and his friends' grand show in *South Pacific*—entertainment by the troops for their peers. There has yet to be established any indication in available military archives as to whether or not the casts or audiences of these shows were integrated, and tracking down the locations of in-camp performances proves an equal challenge. Luther Hanson, the curator of the Army Museum at Fort Lee, realizes that "every military post had at least one theatre for the blacks and one for the whites and sometimes a separate theatre for the women. So there were at least two, possibly three theatres on every base where these plays would have happened."[9]

In 1943 the *Infantry Journal* published the Soldier Shows series and released them to the troops, for performance exclusively "by the United States Army and Navy Personnel for their own entertainment."[10] The *Infantry Journal* was one of the most prominent of the government's war journals in the 1930s and 1940s. Ranging in titles from "So You're Going Overseas!" to "Animal Wildlife of the Pacific," these journals served largely as instructional manuals for young troopers. Luther Hanson reminds us that the *Infantry Journal* was "the infantry's main journal, it was passed out all throughout the country." War Department officer Major John Halpin Burns declared in 1941 that the *Infantry Journal* "now speaks for the Army." In March of 1942 the War Department reconfigured the structure of the combat-arms journals, and all of the publications were produced under the general management of the Requirements Division. "Many feared that the abolition of the [individual] chiefs would threaten troop morale and continuation of the journals but the [Army Ground Forces] soothed everyone by stressing these publications' roles as 'custodians and preservers of esprit.'"[11] The Soldier Shows series were published as a means to this end.

The *Soldier Shows Guide,* in keeping with the journal's tradition, is an exceptionally thorough instructional manual for preparing and presenting productions. The guide details needed personnel and instructions for casting, rehearsal, acting, lighting design, and set construction. In chapter 4 of the guide, "Methods for Procuring Published Scripts: Material Produced by the Special Services Division," the War Department explains, "Material is now being distributed . . . for redistribution to all Army Libraries. . . . A supplementary distribution of this material is made, when practicable, on strength figures, the basis being approximately one copy per every 1500 men, such copies sent to the Special Service Officers of posts and tactical units, here and overseas."[12]

According to the Library of Congress holdings, the *Infantry Journal* released twenty-five publications in 1943. Of these releases, three circulations—*Army Play by Play, Comedy Scenes,* and *Minstrel Show Material*—were released as scripts intended for entertainment and not as instructional guides. In addition to what exists in the Library of Congress archives, the *Soldier Shows Guide* indicates "the following material has been distributed, or will be in the near future." The list includes the three aforementioned scripts and goes on to list *The Monologue Joke Book, The Pocketbook of War Humor,* four volumes of *At Ease*—which bear comedy sketches and songs from successful Broadway shows, minstrel shows, and popular radio sketches—and three volumes simply titled *Soldier Shows,* consisting of comedy sketches and routines compiled by the Committee on Scripts for Soldier and Sailor Shows of the Writer's War Board.

The most notable of these releases, presumably intended to boost morale and race relations among the stationed troops, is the second volume of *At Ease,* which provides "the dialogue for two complete minstrel shows, especially interlocutor and endmen routines,"[13] and Mort Lewis's *Comedy Acts and Minstrel Show Material.* Both texts contain a series of short sketches prepared and produced by Infantry Journal, Inc. Lewis's script reveals the anecdotes of the characters from the *Maxwell House Showboat* radio show "Molasses 'n January," which was largely successful in the South and Southwest. Lewis's *Infantry Journal* script reveals Sergeant January and his dim-witted friend, the unlucky and misunderstood Private Molasses. Molasses hails from the bluntly named Chitlin' Switch, a town so small that "'Welcome' and 'Come Again' are on the same sign" (Lewis, *Comedy Acts,* 38).

It is through the resulting stories of January, Molasses, Molasses's girlfriend, Ducky Pew, and their family and friends, that the stereotypes of black people are predominately exploited and perpetuated. Their stories form the bulk of this text; their jokes range from the common minstrel trademark mispronunciations and imaginative and descriptive character names to genuine insults about physical differences in the black physique and about the black man's general ignorance and backward ways.

In *An American Dilemma: The Negro Problem and Modern Democracy,* Gunnar Myrdal surmises from a series of anthropological studies, of which "the ideal in regard to large number of cases was the Army study" (albeit with its drawbacks) that "compared to the average white man, the average Negro of the present day seems to exhibit the following physical traits: head slightly longer and narrower; . . . nose broader; lips thicker; external ear shorter; nasal depth greater; torso shorter; arms and legs longer; . . . skin with greater amount of pigment; hair wavy, curly, frizzy, or wooly."[14]

Molasses and January are largely those who exhibit (to each other's and the audience's amusement) these physical characteristics. Their "blackness" (or, in Myrdal's terms, "skin with a greater amount of pigment") comes under attack more than any other physical attribute. In "The Dance" we first meet Molasses's girlfriend, Ducky Pew. She greets him with a pointed reference not only to the shorter torso but also his tone, with "Hello, small, dark, and repulsive" (Lewis, *Comedy Acts,* 19). Mockery of the characters' hue continues throughout the text. In "News from Home," January comments that when Molasses looks pale, he seems a "sort of light charcoal" color (ibid., 38). In "Socks Appeal," January is reprimanded about his uniform by a superior:

> EPHUS: That's a pretty black patch you have in the trousers.
> JANUARY: That ain't no patch! (Turns around) That's me! (ibid., 50)

The sketch "Swimming" depicts January approaching Molasses: "Those are big water wings you're wearing" for Molasses to inevitably respond, "Those ain't water wings—those are my shoulder blades!" (ibid., 53). In a separate series of crossfire that underlines the assumptions of blacks' color, intelligence, longer heads, and broader noses, the pair fight:

> JANUARY: Now look here: Are you going to get out of that bed?
> MOLASSES: I will, Sergeant, if you'll promise to put me in the Camouflage Corps. I'd like to act as camouflage.

JANUARY: Why, you leather-headed ape! What sort of camouflage could you act as?
MOLASSES: A smoke screen.
JANUARY: I can see thou getting K.P. duty.
MOLASSES: Oh, Sergeant, how can a young, handsome looking Sergeant be so crew-el? A Sergeant with down on your cheeks.
JANUARY: What's down on my cheeks?
MOLASSES: The bags under your eyes.
JANUARY: Don't you start making cracks about my looks. What's wrong about my looks? Look at that broad nose. Your nose is so broad, you have to wear your glasses side-saddle! Boy, what a nose!
MOLASSES: What you're breathing through ain't no freckle! (ibid., 72)

When January and Molasses do not bear the brunt of these physical gags, Molasses refers to his cousins as the subject of his storytelling. The result is the reference to his black relatives from and stationed all over the world, proving to the audiences that it is not merely Molasses who exhibits these characteristics but that they are endemic to all black men. Molasses informs us, "My cousin who's in the Pacific with the Army has the biggest ears I ever seed. . . . Last week they had an air raid and he ran as fast as he could to get to the shelter . . . but his ears are so big, they lifted him into the air, and in five minutes he brought down three pigeons, two crows, and a Jap Zero!" (ibid., 19).

In "The G-Man" audiences are entertained with the following anecdote:

JANUARY: Molasses, how is your cousin Polecat Pete?
MOLASSES: You know, he had a funny thing happen to him: he got shot up. They had to give him a transfusion fast and the only thing around was a bull dog, so they gave him a transfusion from the bull dog.
JANUARY: Transfusion from a bull dog? Is there anything peculiar about him?
MOLASSES: Oh yeah—he goes out all day chasing cats!
JANUARY: Boy, is that a terrible thing to happen.
MOLASSES: Yeah, they shot off most of his hair on his head, too, and they had to graft fur from an animal on to his head.
JANUARY: The fur of what animal did they put on his head?
MOLASSES: I ain't sure, but every time he gets excited, they have to bury his clothes! (ibid., 24)

This specific sketch references both the unfortunate fact that blood donations were segregated and that black blood supplies were poorly maintained. It also derives its humor by proposing that cousin Polecat Pete had such shadowy and substantial hair that the best match for him was the dark, thick fur of a skunk.

Potentially more offensive than the War Department's encouraging reinforcement of the U.S. Army's established physical differences in Negroes are the social stereotypes perpetuated in the *Minstrel Show Material* pages. The U.S. Army's findings did include that black men had smaller cranial cavities, but this fact had never been linked to proving inferior intellectual capacity in blacks. Lewis's script, however, reminds the troops otherwise. In "The Truth Gong" January congratulates Molasses for a good idea, expressing his shock as he reminds Molasses, "you're naturally so dumb" (Lewis, *Comedy Acts,* 64). In "The Work House" Molasses stops to get a room for the night, proclaiming to January, the "clerk," "I saw a sign outside that said 'Work House.' I have stopped at the Ritz House Hotel and the Waldorf House and I figures this Work House was a good hotel." January then speaks to the audience: "He thinks this jail is a hotel. You is the dumbest fellow I ever saw" (ibid., 68). Molasses's lack of intelligence allows a dual reading here: his Negro ignorance lands him in jail.

In the pages of this script blacks are not merely physically categorized for mockery; traits that were socially considered endemic to black men (particularly in the minds of southern whites) are also used as comical fodder in *Minstrel Show Material.* The notion that blacks are dirty, are largely criminals, and have no sense of social grace are all given voice in Lewis's script. Possibly the tamest assault is that blacks are socially ignorant of manners and propriety. In "Proposal" Molasses wants to propose to Ducky Pew but doesn't know how to get on her best side to do so. January suggests he "go to see her all dressed up." Molasses protests and asks his friend, "You mean I has to wear socks?" because, he admits, "I ain't much for formal wear" (ibid., 45). In a separate account Molasses goes on to wrongfully extol the story of another cousin in "He Sunk a U-Boat," proving again his own ignorance and the notion that blacks were inclined toward criminal behavior:

MOLASSES: You know my cousin Absorbine Senior?
JANUARY: Yeah.
MOLASSES: Well, every tenant of the place he lives in wrote to the man what runs the building?
JANUARY: Every tenant of the place wrote to the man what runs the building?
MOLASSES: Yeah. They wrote, "It's a shame, that when the Government needs it, you keeps so much iron stuff around here. Tear down the iron fences around the place and finally we ask you to remove the unsightly iron work in every room and give it all to the Government."
JANUARY: Did the man who ran the place do it?
MOLASSES: No. The Warden refused. (ibid., 31)

Reasserting the notion that blacks are naturally unclean, in "First Aid" Molasses tells us:

MOLASSES: You know, my gal Ducky Pew, she knitted a sweater for my dirty cousin Grit who's in the army.
JANUARY: Your dirty cousin Grit?
MOLASSES: Yes. You know, he and the sweater are so much alike.
JANUARY: How?
MOLASSES: They both shrink from washing. (ibid., 21)

This material is not indicative of the other minstrel material being produced nationwide. Although *Amos 'n Andy* was still broadcast on the radio, minstrel acts were experiencing a decline relative to more spectacular variety shows. Whereas many of the contemporaneous minstrel show scripts maintained the traditional style and format, by the 1920s the texts largely moved away from specifically attacking blacks and relied more on universal misfortunes and misunderstandings. American popular culture saw a significant decrease in blackface performance in the 1930s, and the trend away from the more derogatory material continued into the next decade. In Hollywood the "movement towards more positive portrayals of blacks was confirmed in 1942 when senior Hollywood executives met delegates of the National Association for the Advancement of Colored People. At this meeting an agreement was reached whereby the studios agreed to abandon pejorative racial roles."[15]

With a national trend toward disassociation from a negative, racially stereotypical performance history, it appears even more noteworthy that the U.S. War Department, steeped in concerns and complaints from troops dealing with racial conflicts and pressured by the president and Washington leaders to assuage irregular and unjustified racial disparity, would willingly release material that was rife with blatant attacks on black soldiers. This is especially notable because the War Department concurrently released universally comic material that emphasized the more common situations of the stationed men. It is important to recognize the War Department's desire to bring minstrel shows as popular entertainment to the camps, especially since the shows would have been popular with southern war officials; the material is not, however, representative of the contemporary American trends in its treatment of racial representation.

Equally interesting are the disparate messages delivered to the troops within the same time frame. In 1943 both the initial Soldier Shows scripts and the *Educational Program for Colored Troops* pamphlet were released. The *Educational Program* directive was "handed out . . . to bri-

gade, group, and battalion commanders and officers of Negro units."
It stated, "Generalities about Negroes, as about everything else, are usually inaccurate." This message is in obvious conflict with the content of
the *Minstrel Show Material*'s pages, despite the War Department's endorsement of both publications. The same edict also decreed the following moral mantra: "A good soldier doesn't have time to fool with
his hometown politics. . . . Any question about white people and black
people will never be settled by barracks talk. Let's forget about these
things for the time being and buckle down to real soldiering and win
this war."[16]

The irony here is that the *Comedy Acts and Minstrel Show Material*
and the second volume of *At Ease* were distributed to the men for their
personal entertainment, enabling them to take this material into their
barracks and to laugh over it with their peers. The content of these
pages reiterate the ideas perpetuated through the southern "hometown
politics" into which black soldiers found themselves repositioned. If the
intent of these journal releases was to appease the troops and to boost
their morale, why would the War Department enable the *Infantry Journal*, a self-proclaimed mouthpiece for the army, to publish and distribute
such racially charged and discriminatory material?

Daniel Kryder cites the summer of 1943 as the height of cultural disturbances between troops:

> disaffection among black soldiers peaked in mid-1943. . . . In early summer,
> blacks and whites fought in Camp Stewart, Georgia, March Field, Califor-
> nia, Camp Bliss, Texas, and Camp Breckinridge, Kentucky. The disorders
> of 1943 seemed to follow a new pattern: As in the Camp Stewart case, they
> were more likely to occur inside a camp, often between identifiable military
> units, and were as likely to be caused by blacks as by whites.[17]

Although pinpointing the release date of the Soldier Show scripts has
proved an enormous challenge, an announcement in the *New York Times*
for the return engagement of the Second Service Command's production of *Army Play by Play*, opening at the Martin Beck on July 26, 1943
(with the initial performance at the Forty-sixth Street theatre on June
14), and a program for a production of *Army Play by Play* at the Wor-
chester Auditorium in September of 1943 indicate that the scripts would
have been released at least in April or May.[18] Each of the racial disturbances to which Kryder refers took place in June, July, and August. It
is difficult to believe, even if the integrated troops enjoying these performances were without racial prejudice, that the in-your-face assertion
of these stereotypes would not incite some form of conflict. The common act of repeating a favorite humorous line later in the evening (or

month), perhaps over drinks in a newly integrated post bar, would have only added to the racial tensions that provoked in-camp disturbances. I believe that these events require simultaneous recognition and that the concurrence of the *Comedy Acts and Minstrel Show Material* and *At Ease* (volume 2) releases and the accounts of in-camp race riots would have affected one another.

It is also my concern that the War Department's intent for the production of these materials may be more influenced by minstrel history than previously realized. Geery Floyd, a historian at the Fort Bliss Infantry Museum explained, "sometimes the blacks would go into the white clubs to entertain the guys."[19] This fact enables an especially significant reading of the only self-referential line in Lewis's minstrel play. In "The G-Man," when January provokes Molasses's fear of dying, Molasses exclaims, "I don't want to be no ghost in blackface" (Lewis, *Comedy Acts,* 24). In the *Soldier Shows Guide,* under the instructions for "Practical Devices for Make-Up," the following appears: "MINSTREL MAKE-UP. Negro make-up is very simple. Burnt cork is probably the easiest. The actor must be sure he has applied cold cream before the burnt cork is put on. Black grease paint will probably go on more evenly than the burnt cork. The mouth should be enlarged by red or white grease paint or moist rouge. White spaces are left around the eyes to make them appear larger."[20]

This raises the most obvious question and concern: were the *Comedy Acts and Minstrel Show Material* and the second volume of *At Ease* intended for blacks to perform, in blackface, for white troops? The military's instructions do not specifically promote the casting of either whites or blacks in these roles, yet the mere encouragement of whites continuing to perform in blackface (while simultaneously training with black troops) would produce detrimental effects on morale. It is clear that this blackface performance was the intent of the *Infantry Journal*'s publications and that the War Department in 1943, despite its few pacifying and conciliatory publications, frankly favored the perpetuation of negative racial stereotypes, again, "due in large part to its reputed domination by white southern personnel." The department's publication of *At Ease* (volume 2) and *Comedy Acts and Minstrel Show Material,* the content within their pages, and the strict instruction given for blackface minstrel performance underscore the truth of this claim.

Notes

1. Harvard Sitkoff, "African American Militancy in the World War II South: Another Perspective," in *Remaking Dixie: The Impact of World War II*

on the American South, ed. Neil R. McMillen (Jackson: University Press of Mississippi, 1997), 74.

2. Daniel Kryder, *Divided Arsenal: Race and the American State during World War II* (New York: Cambridge University Press, 1990), 70.

3. Ulysses Lee, *The Employment of Negro Troops* (Washington, DC: Center of Military History, United States Army, 1990), 373.

4. Kryder, *Divided Arsenal,* 136.

5. Phillip McGuire, *Taps for a Jim Crow Army: Letters from Black Soldiers in World War II* (Santa Barbara, CA: ABC-Clio Press, 1983), 171.

6. Kryder, *Divided Arsenal,* 161, 171.

7. "Patriotic Revue Proves Marvelous Morale-Builder," *Pittsburgh Courier,* June 5, 1943, microform collection, Auburn Avenue Research Library, Atlanta, no page number available.

8. War Department, Special Services Division, Army Service Force. *Soldier Show's Guide* (Washington, DC: Infantry Journal, 1943), 10:8.

9. Luther Hanson, phone interview by the author, March 26, 2005.

10. Mort Lewis, *Comedy Acts and Minstrel Show Material* (Washington, DC: Infantry Journal, 1943), 2. Subsequent references to this volume will be cited within the body of the text.

11. Leslie Anders, "Retrospect: Four Decades of American Military Journalism," *Military Affairs* 41, no. 2 (April 1977): 62–67.

12. War Department, Special Services Division, Army Service Force, *Soldier Show's Guide* (Washington, DC: Infantry Journal, 1943), 10:45.

13. Ibid.

14. Gunnar Myrdal, *An American Dilemma: The Negro Problem and Modern Democracy* (New York: Harper and Brothers, 1944), 1:139.

15. Peter Stanfield, "'An Octoroon in the Kindling': American Vernacular and Blackface Minstrelsy in 1930s Hollywood," *Journal of American Studies* 31 (1997): 408.

16. "'Education for Negro Troops' Pamphlet Issued at Camp Stewart Is Contradictory," *People's Voice,* Aug. 28, 1943, clipping file, archives, Fort Stewart Museum Collection, Fort Stewart Georgia. No page number available.

17. Kryder, *Divided Arsenal,* 146.

18. "Soldier Show Here Soon for 2 Weeks," *New York Times,* July 12, 1943; *Army Play by Play,* program for Monday, Sep. 27, 1943, collection of the author.

19. Geery Floyd, phone interview by the author, March 26, 2005.

20. War Department, *Soldier Show's Guide,* 119.

In the Jungle of Cities

May '68 Arrives in Avignon

Kate Bredeson

I N MAY 1968 PARIS exploded as workers and students united in protest, seizing the streets and halting everyday life. School and work were put on pause as debates spilled out onto Seine-side boulevards; sidewalks became the stages for riots and impromptu performances. Theatre was central to the May '68 revolution, and, with the occupation of the Odéon, the revolution's center became a theatre. From the dramatic slogans and graffiti that covered Paris's stone walls to the staged marches of thousands and the presence of the Living Theatre, the entire month was one enormous theatrical event.

But as Kristin Ross notes in *May '68 and Its Afterlives,* the spectacle of the May events extended beyond the borders of Paris and the confines of one month.[1] Far south of Paris, the final dramas of May '68 were embodied, enacted, and exorcised in Avignon during the famous summer festival. In Lenora Champagne's words, "Avignon was the battleground where the cultural revolution aspects of May continued to be fought through the summer."[2] That the festival was held at all was a feat, as most other French festivals, notably Cannes, had been cancelled. But Avignon artistic director Jean Vilar defiantly prevailed, despite the withdrawal of all but two scheduled acts as a result of May-related production problems.

Two firecracker events started the proverbial bonfires that consumed the south of France that summer. A pair of plays promoting visions of utopia, *La paillasse aux seins nus,* by Gérard Gelas, and *Paradise Now,* by the Living Theatre, were banned, the first before it was ever seen and the second after three performances. The censorship of *Paradise Now* has become a source of legend. But it was the ban of nineteen-year-old Gelas's play, produced with his company the Chêne Noir, that provoked the onslaught of riots and debates. The ban of Gelas's play has become a footnote in the history of the Living Theatre, but without its censorship the atmosphere in Avignon wouldn't have reached the boiling point that enabled the ban of the American troupe.

La paillasse aux seins nus was the Chêne Noir's first full-length play. Gelas founded the company, whose name means "Black Oak," in 1966 after dropping out of film school. The Chêne Noir spent its first year giving performances of poetry and music at a local Avignon restaurant called the Poule au Pot. The performances were inspired by musicians such as John Coltrane, Charles Mingus, Ravi Shankar, and Pierre Henry, as well as by André Benedetto's play *Napalm*, which was performed at the 1967 Festival d'Avignon. The end of the troupe's first performance featured Coltrane's song "A Love Supreme" accompanied by voices chanting, "Liberté . . . liberté . . . anarchie . . . liberté."[3] After his experiences at the Poule au Pot, Gelas knew he wanted to make theatre, a different kind of theatre from what he grew up seeing: "At the end of the 'Poule au Pot' period, my decision was made. It was necessary to make theater, a different theater with comrades."[4] He was drawn toward political performance, collective creation, and anarchic expression. Gelas completed writing *La paillasse aux seins nus* in March 1968, and rehearsals began the first week of May. Although not officially a part of the Avignon festival, the play was to be staged concurrently in a former bomb shelter across the river from downtown.

Rumors began circulating about Gelas's play long before it opened. The play's title alone announced it as provocative: *paillasse* means "straw mattress" but also "cheap prostitute." *Seins nus* means "bare breasts." But the play is hardly a tawdry skin show; the plot is a simple love story that begins when a young man, Jean, meets a woman, Crevure, in a Seine-side bar. The whole of the play happens in one night, unfolds in real time, and features a cast of motley types who wander in and out of the bar. There is a bartender, a beatnik, a vagrant named Pierrot, and even the Seine itself appears as a character. Though there are no stage directions, Gelas manages to convey via dialogue a thick, hazy atmosphere of seediness and dilapidation. The bar, like its inhabitants, is musty, tired, and downtrodden. Conversely, Gelas's language is heightened and decorous though peppered with slang. Punctuation is irregular, and the words are arranged on the page so that the text looks more like a poem than a play. In the opening scene Crevure asks Jean his name, and he replies: "What could knowing that do to you?" She replies: "Make me hot, make me cold. Neither hot nor cold. Sun. Spring. Snow." He answers: "Revolution. Perdition. Exclamation. Suction."[5]

Gelas remembers eating breakfast at home with his parents on the morning of July 18, the day his play was set to open, when suddenly the police arrived and took him away in a paddy wagon. At the station he was read a police order banning his play on grounds that it would "gravely trouble public order or public tranquillity."[6] Gelas was ordered to take down all posters advertising the play. Soon thereafter, his parents' house was ransacked by the police, who seized his personal letters, books, and poems. With the police ban of the play, he remembers, "The first punch of the Festival d'Avignon fight was thrown."[7]

How was a love story presented by a fledgling theatre company composed of teenagers so able to "gravely trouble public order" that it had to be stopped? The play depicts no acts of violence, no mass uprisings, no graphic sex. No one throws a paving stone, no police are beaten, no barricades are constructed. What it does portray is a group of young people engaged in debate. The play flaunts youth, disparages the old regime, and discusses Alfred Jarry, the black power movement, feminism, Vietnam, the Compagnies républicaines de sécurité (CRS) French riot police, and the questioned existence of God. It also references the French Revolution, the Paris Commune, and the Algerian War. Ultimately, it depicts the founding of a new world. Both a funeral mass and a wedding party, the play is a celebration of the demise of one era and the ascent of another, the new era marked by action in lieu of passivity, by creation instead of withering.

Gelas makes the river at Paris's heart into a female character, and she is the most outraged, wise, and provocative figure in the play. She poses the most dangerous questions to fellow characters and audience members alike. She is the voice of reason, the lifeline who has seen and connects all. In the middle of the play she launches into an exhausted diatribe against Jean, the Beatnik, and the consumer society in which these two men dwell:

> But really, finally, do you find it normal to have women selling themselves to men who buy them, . . . to have military chiefs or presidents, or both at the same time, taking rides in cars full of CRSS UWXYZ who follow them to beat those who slave away all day long? . . . So do you find it normal to be galloping towards universal fascism? . . . DO YOU FIND THAT NORMAL, DO YOU?[8]

One famous poster to emerge from the École des Beaux-Arts in May depicts a herd of sheep all facing one direction, with the slogan *Retour à la normale* [Return to normal] looming above. There was a great sense of fear among leftists and all who had fought in the streets that once the movement started losing strength, all the momentum, power, and spectacle of May would be forgotten and that everything would go back to how it had been. Gelas, writing in March, already voiced the concerns of post-May fighters.

In his play the exterior world gallops toward fascism, yet at the same time the one inside the bar is made anew, and done so in a distinctly Shakespearean fashion: the formation and marriage of two couples—Jean and Crevure, the Beatnik and the Seine. The Seine explains the double wedding, "It's to remake life, to remake society. WE'RE FED UP!"[9] Tired of the sick exterior society, this awkward quartet creates a new one.

Within a forty-one-page text Gelas prophetically crafted the kind of dialogue and reverie prevalent in Paris in May. From the Odéon to the discussion groups formed across the country, debate fueled the May events. Talk was revolution. In Gelas's play a group of youth meet, talk passionately, and carry out a new world order. This kind of talk terrified old-guard authority in post-May France. In Paris police were dispatched to patrol any areas where youth might gather: museums, cafés, theatres, cinemas; when groups of more than three assembled, they were ordered to disperse. In the end the hope evident in *La paillasse* lies in the paltry group of misfits and the epic dreams they share. In Gelas's world society at large is going to hell, but a small circle holds the power to make change and start anew.

There is no evidence that any civic official read *La paillasse aux seins nus* before censoring it. Yet the title, coupled with the knowledge of the playwright's politics, was enough to shut down the performance. Once the news was delivered, the spectacle that followed was probably more dramatic and chaotic than anything that would have been inspired by the play's staging. As journalist Christian Maurel wrote following the ban, "[T]he unknown anarchist troupe the Chêne Noir would be, without even wanting to, the spark that lit the fires."[10]

On the night when *La paillasse* was to have opened, the former bomb-shelter cave where the play was to be performed was surrounded by guards, and the bridge leading to it was occupied on either end by CRS agents with machine guns. The Living Theatre canceled its scheduled performance of *Antigone* and took the stage with festival director Jean Vilar and the Chêne Noir, holding a dialogue with the audience that lasted until 3:00 a.m. The next night, festival headliner Maurice Béjart's dance company performed the aptly titled *Mass for the Present Time*. During the last tableau the members of the Chêne Noir were invited onstage, where they stretched out across the stage floor. A representative of the company spoke: "We are the Chêne Noir. Why ban our theatre?

Why is the text of the play banned in all of France?"[11] Béjart's troupe created one of the most dramatic images of that summer as they danced among the sprawled, banned bodies.

In the end the Chêne Noir enjoyed far more stage time than they would have had they performed in their cave across the river. For the July 20 representation of *Antigone* the Living Theatre performed while the black-clad Chêne Noir company sat onstage in a row, their backs resting on the upstage wall, staring at the audience, their mouths taped over with large rectangles of blue, white, and red in the image of the French flag. The Chêne Noir sat still throughout the performance as the Living Theatre enacted Judith Malina's version of the young woman who stands up to authority. Gelas said of the whole experience, for his troupe's first professional endeavor, it was a "Glorieux début."[12]

Gérard Gelas and the Chêne Noir never saw their play reach the stage in 1968. But the events of that summer made Gelas a famous playwright and director even though no one saw his premiere. Following that summer, the Chêne Noir became a fixture of the Avignon theatre community; today the company is the community's pillar. *La paillasse aux seins nus* has never had a full production, but in October 2002, to mark the thirty-fifth anniversary of the Chêne Noir, the play was given a staged reading, its first-ever public appearance. Gelas, current artistic director of the Chêne Noir, located a copy of the script in Daniel Auteuil's mother's attic. Auteuil, today one of France's most popular film stars, returned to his hometown to read the part of Jean, which he was supposed to have performed in 1968. The event was described by the actors, director, and the local press as highly emotional for everyone involved, especially Gelas and the original cast members who returned to read the roles they had never been able to play. For the Chêne Noir, who have continued to produce provocative and political theatre, including 2001's *Guantanamour*, the event was fitting: "after 35 years, the Chêne remains faithful to their rebellious youth."[13]

Paradise Lost: The Living Theatre at Avignon

The Chêne Noir was not the only company to enjoy a "glorious debut" in Avignon in 1968. The Living Theatre unveiled its new work, *Paradise Now,* during the festival. With that premiere, as well as the melee that followed, *France nouvelle* correspondent Edith Rappaport noted, "The Living Theatre has become, under the cover of the May events, the symbol of the 1968 Festival d'Avignon."[14]

The American anarchist-pacifist company already enjoyed fame in France for its early productions and was invited to Avignon to perform

Mysteries and Smaller Pieces, Antigone, and a new creation of its choice. Following time in the south of France, the company planned its first return to the United States in four years and a tour of the new performance. At the end of April the company arrived unannounced and penniless in Avignon, weeks ahead of schedule. After the troupe was kicked out of a hotel, Vilar's assistant Paul Puaux arranged for members to stay in a local high school. The troupe was paid in full up front for its contracted twenty-one performances and quickly settled in: Gérard Gelas recalls helping paint the walls of the high school and decorating the rooms with brightly colored paper, as well as chalk slogans such as "révolution," "amour," "indiens," "guérilla," and "rite."[15] Many troupe members dyed their sheets black, saying they couldn't sleep on white sheets and that they wanted their bedding to look like anarchy flags. They were the only Americans scheduled to perform; the other dramatic pieces in the lineup were all French, including a Théâtre National Populaire (TNP)-produced *Le diable et le bon Dieu,* the Théâtre Montparnasse's *Le concile d'amour,* Antoine Bourseiller's staging of Jean-Claude van Italie's *America Hurrah,* and a production of Baudelaire's *Crénom.*

On June 8 Vilar announced that all of the French companies had dropped out because the May strikes had prevented rehearsals and production planning. That left only Maurice Béjart's dance company, the Living Theatre, and several film and music offerings. In late June Vilar held a press conference announcing the changes to the schedule and proclaiming the 1968 festival a celebration of "free discussion," an opportunity to engage in dialogue about the recent events.

Throughout June and July people who weren't necessarily performers, journalists, or spectators flowed into Avignon. Groups of rowdy agitators, called *enragés,* from Paris filled the streets, and some of them moved into the Lycée Mistral, bunking with the Living Theatre. The town square became an outdoor Odéon of the south, a drop-in center for constant conversation and provocation ruled by many who had been expelled from the Parisian theatre only weeks before. On the opening night of the festival the *enragés* staged a large protest to, as Alfred Simon noted, make the Avignon people and the festival goers "understand that the festival could not take place as if the barricades of May '68 hadn't been built."[16] They called the festival a "supermarché de la culture" [supermarket of culture].[17] The townspeople were shocked by the eclectic dress and lifestyle of the newcomers. Provençal newspapers were splashed with gratuitous photos of the Living Theatre company members and their followers. They were depicted as straggle-haired, baby-toting hippies dressed in Indian fabrics and beads. An article in

Le nouvel observateur reported that "the Avignon people thought they'd seen the arrival of Satan-worshippers."[18]

Local authorities were becoming concerned about the influx of rowdy youth and about rumors of potentially inflammatory programming at the festival. Vilar met with town officials several times; they ultimately secured a promise that the police would not interfere with anything surrounding the festival or the invited performers without first consulting the festival administration. By this point the atmosphere in the city was electric. Everyone was aware that any minor scuffle could start a potentially violent brawl. Judith Malina remembers, "The feeling in Avignon was that we were on the brink of a volcanic revolution."[19]

Following the ban of Gelas's play, as well as several well-received performances of *Antigone*, *Paradise Now* opened in Avignon on July 24 to a full house. There was a tremendous atmosphere of anticipation surrounding the new work, which had been produced in total secrecy. Vilar wasn't allowed in rehearsals. Beck said that if Artaud, his spiritual mentor, was alive, even he would have been kept away.

The Living Theatre developed the idea for *Paradise Now* while in Cefalù, Italy. There they spent time reading and discussing philosophy, history, and religion, as well as practicing yoga and meditation. *Paradise Now* evolved out of these exchanges and experiences. The troupe had lofty aspirations for its new piece: "For *Paradise Now*, Julian wanted to devise a form that could allow the release of spontaneous creative forces which could transform audiences and society."[20] They wanted a work that would evolve and change, depending on where it was performed and for whom. What wouldn't change was the ultimate radical goal of the work: "The act would project a revolutionary situation and lay the groundwork for anarchist action cells which would begin the work of revolution."[21] The desired revolution was not purely physical but spiritual, as well; the company described *Paradise Now* as

a voyage from the many to one and from the one to the many. It's a spiritual voyage and a political voyage. It is an interior voyage and an exterior voyage. It is a voyage for the actors and the spectators. It begins in the present and moves into the future and returns to the present. The plot is The Revolution. The voyage is a vertical ascent toward the Permanent Revolution.[22]

The "Revolution" that the Living Theatre described "is the beautiful, nonviolent, anarchist revolution. The purpose of the play is to lead to a state of being in which nonviolent revolutionary action is possible."[23] The play's "script" is a hand-drawn chart that resembles a ladder composed of eight rungs. Each rung contains a "rite," a "vision," and an "action." The rites and visions are performed by the company; the actions are led by the actors, with the goal that they will be performed primarily by the audiences. The first half of *Paradise Now* is composed of a series of key phrases: "I am not allowed to travel without a passport!" "I don't know how to stop the wars!" "You can't live if you don't have money!" "I'm not allowed to take my clothes off!" (In Avignon, these statements were delivered in French.) This part of the spectacle intends to show the world in its current state. After the fifth tableau the violent, restrictive realm of today transforms into a world of nonviolence; the second half of *Paradise Now* illustrates the paths that can lead to revolution and paradise.

On the opening night of *Paradise Now* more than five hundred people waited near the theatre gates, trying to get in. The performance started at 10:00 p.m. and culminated in an early-morning procession through the streets, with the company and the audience yelling, "The theater is in the street. The street belongs to the people. Free the theater. Free the street. Begin."[24] The street parade was key to Beck and Malina's goal. The end of the performance offers the spectator the chance to apply what he or she has experienced; the company leads them directly outside of the theater walls into the world in need of change. In their twenty years as performers, at no time were the members of the Living Theatre closer to achieving revolution than in the wake of May 1968.

Reactions to *Paradise Now* varied widely. There was a lot of confusion, like the technicians who asked Vilar why the actors weren't allowed to eat chickpeas (they misheard "haschisch" as "pois chiches" during the line: "Je veux du haschisch" [I want hashish]. Many spectators loved it and joined the company onstage. Many weren't able to get into the theatre; some protested the admission charge. The neighbors near the theatre hated being kept awake until 3:00 a.m. by the performance, which was dominated not by words but by wailing. The critics' reactions varied—ranging from high praise to disgust. Réjane Tronel in *Le dauphine libéré* enthusiastically declared, "The Living Theatre is crazy, but what theater! And what a document of this era."[25] *Le Figaro*'s correspondent, Claude Baignères, simply stated, "The Festival d'Avignon is dead."[26]

Paradise Now played three times in Avignon. The troupe was scheduled to continue for another two performances, and Beck announced a free performance in a pubic square for Saturday, July 28. But on the afternoon of July 27 the mayor of Avignon, Henri Duffaut, met with Beck and told the company to replace the remaining scheduled stagings of *Paradise Now* with either *Mysteries and Smaller Pieces* or *Antigone*.

According to Duffaut the reasons for the ban were contractual; he said Beck and company breached their contract, which specified that they would play only within the walls of the theater. He also refused to allow a public performance because "forcing" a spectacle on an unwitting audience would be a "viol des consciences" [violation of conscience].[27] Beck left the meeting in agreement not to perform *Paradise Now* again but said he would return the next to day to discuss its replacement, after talking with his company. Duffaut gave a press conference that night, explaining the contract violation and subsequent ban.

For Beck, Malina, and company the ban was a blatant act of censorship. They had discussed the possibility that *Paradise Now* would be banned because of its politics and nudity, but they hadn't anticipated being censored for wanting to perform for free. The group found especially heinous, given *Antigone*'s politics, the idea of staging *Antigone* in lieu of an outlawed play. They decided to withdraw from the festival.

On the evening of July 28 Beck read an eleven-point statement, an announcement and explanation of why the company had decided to leave the festival. The artist collective l'Atelier Populaire reproduced paragraph number seven, made it into a poster reminiscent of the École des Beaux-Arts May '68 graphics, and pasted it on walls throughout the city. It read, "Because the time has come for us at last to begin to refuse to serve those who do not want the knowledge and power of art to belong to any but those who can pay for it, who wish to keep the people in the dark, who work for the Power Elite, who wish to control the life of the artist and the lives of people."[28]

Malina remembers being awakened at the high school on July 30 by armed police who "tried to cut" the men's long hair and threw the troupe out of the school.[29] Vilar appeared as well, horrified by Duffaut's actions and apologizing to Beck. Later that day, as the Living Theatre's Volkswagens pulled away from town, a mob assembled to send them off with sympathetic applause and supportive cheers. The mayor celebrated their departure by throwing a citywide party, including a city-sponsored free outdoor dance performance by Maurice Béjart.

That night more than one hundred people crammed the narrow street leading up to the Papal Palace, hoping to block access to Béjart's performance. Police opened up hoses on the crowd to try to disperse them. By then, the Living Theatre was on its way to Chateauvallon, in central France, to perform *Paradise Now*. The town had no idea how big the event would be. The troupe stayed in Chateauvallon for three days; an estimated five thousand people from across the country saw them perform.

According to some critics and spectators, the 1968 Festival d'Avignon

was a resounding failure. But it was actually a remarkably successful festival in terms of financial gains, press coverage, and programming feats.
Vilar considered the 1968 festival a particular coup because so many had
pressed him to cancel it in its entirety after the May events. But he
noted, "After all, during the French Revolution, between 89 and 95, the
theaters played every night."[30] Throughout the spring and summer
events Vilar was the only artistic director who followed in the footsteps
of his French predecessors during the Revolution and the Commune,
and kept his theater open during a time of revolt.

Avignon was a final flare-up of the events of May; by the time the
festival wrapped up, autumn was in the air and France, though still experiencing periodic outbursts, was beginning the return to normality
that so many of the militants had dreaded. Schools reopened, stores
were restocked, new officials were reelected, and theaters opened with
new seasons. In Paris the cobblestones had been cleared and the streets
repaved. As Edith Rappaport noted, quoting Artaud, Avignon served
as a turning point: "With 'Paradise Now' (like the May events), 'theater
arrived at a point where it was necessary for some things to die out in
order to redistribute and begin again.' All is razed: actors, spectators
are put in question. No more written works, roles, house or stage. The
very notion of performance is threatened."[31]

Nowhere were the imminent changes in theater more apparent than
in Avignon in July. From there the Living Theatre took its version of
paradise all over the world, leaving a wake of outrage and excitement.
The next year at Avignon, another collective troupe, the Théâtre du
Soleil, was in residence, practicing its organic political spectacle for the
first time on an international stage. The dramaturgy and practices of
the Chêne Noir and Living Theatre exemplify the mid-1960s shift away
from the Theatre of the Absurd, toward a more actively political, collectively produced theater. May '68 rattled not only the political establishment but the established theater, setting the stage for new dramatic
trends and practices.

But more than anything else, Avignon in 1968 was a laboratory where
the May events were able to be worked out physically. In Paris in May
the theater was a tool for protesters to make their voices heard, one
weapon used in a larger revolution. There theater was a method of expression, a means of protest, and a place to meet and debate. In Avignon
in July the theater was more than a tool—it was the whole backdrop
for and mechanism of dissent. The events of May were boiled down in
Avignon, where the festival was the canvas onto which all of May's unfinished business was projected: that unfinished business included the
fights between students and police, art and government, free expression

and state control. Gelas aptly summed up the summer as a time of confusion and compared the July events to an exorcism: "the situation was extremely complex, confusing, Avignon was a boiling pot at the bottom of which a gigantic psychodrama was playing itself out. The goal, the function: to exorcise May '68 from right to left."[32]

Christian Maurel likened 1968 Avignon to an epic play, with a list of dramatis personae that included the people, the notables, the *enragés,* the dancers, the police, the fascists, the mistral, the "living," the Chêne Noir, the Communist Party, and the pope (Vilar). He compares the festival itself to a sprawling piece of theater: "For the first time in Avignon, the spectacle wasn't only onstage. It was everywhere, in the streets, in the shadow of city hall, the prefecture, the police stations. The play is political. It's called 'In the jungle of Avignon, or the festival of fear.' Everyone performs in it."[33] Maurel even includes the strong southerly winds ("le mistral") as a character; everyone, and everything, in the city was implicated in the grand drama of Avignon 1968, and the events took on the feeling of a Greek tragedy.

Avignon signaled the definitive arrival of collectively based, actively political theatre. The Chêne Noir purged the events of May via slicing verbal attacks on the broken French system; the Living Theatre did so even more physically, channeling their rage, disillusion, and hope by shaking their bare bodies and bellowing primal screams. On an international stage these two troupes debated, trembled, and shouted out the anger and unsatiated idealism of May. In the end it was by way of these two banned companies that the Festival d'Avignon effected the conclusion to May most suitable to the drama that it had become: catharsis.

Notes

1. Kristin Ross, *May '68 and Its Afterlives* (Chicago: University of Chicago Press, 2002). This argument is a refrain in Ross's book.

2. Lenora Champagne, *French Theatre Experiment since 1968* (Ann Arbor: UMI Research Press, 1984), 21.

3. Gérard Gelas, *Théâtre du Chêne Noir: Essais et documents* (Paris: Editions Stock, 1972), 15.

4. "A la fin de la période de la 'Poule au Pot,' ma décision était prise. Il fallait faire du théâtre, un autre théâtre avec des frères" (Gelas, *Théâtre,* 13). Unless otherwise noted, all translations of passages taken from Gelas's book are mine.

5. The French script reads as follows:

JEAN: Qu'est-ce que ça peut vous faire?
CREVURE: Me faire chaud, me faire froid. Ni chaud ni froid. Soleil. Printemps. Neige.
JEAN: Révolution. Perdition. Exclamation. Succion.

Gérard Gelas, *La paillasse aux seins nus* (unpublished; text provided courtesy of Gelas), 1.
6. "est susceptible de troubler gravement l'ordre public ou la tranquillité publique" (Gelas, *Théâtre*, 43).
7. "Le coup d'envoi de la contestation du Festival d'Avignon est donné" (Gelas, *Théâtre*, 37).
8. "Mais enfin, quand même, vous trouvez ça normal d'avoir des femmes qui se vendent à des hommes qui les achètent, . . . d'avoir des chefs militaires ou présidents, ou les deux à la fois, qui se baladent avec des bagnoles pleines de CRSS UWXYZ qui les suivent pour cogner sur ceux qui triment toute la journée? . . . Alors vous trouver ça normal qu'on galope comme ça vers le fascisme universel? . . . VOUS TROUVEZ ÇA NORMAL, VOUS?" (Gelas, *La paillasse*, 23).
9. "C'est pour refaire la vie, refaire la société. ON EN A MARRE!" (Gelas, *La paillasse*, 26).
10. "la troupe inconnue et anarchiste du 'Chêne Noir,' va être, sans le vouloir, l'étincelle qui met le feu aux poudres" (Christian Maurel, "Notre époque: Le Micro-mai d'Avignon," *Le nouvel observateur*, July 29–Aug. 4, 1968).
11. "Nous sommes du théâtre du Chêne Noir. Pourquoi interdit-on notre théâtre? Pourquoi le texte de la pièce est-il interdit dans toute la France?" quoted in Jean-Claude Bardot, *Jean Vilar* (Paris: Armand Colin, 1991), 508.
12. Gelas, *Théâtre*, 39.
13. "à 35 ans, le Chêne s'affiche toujours fidèle à sa jeunesse rebelle" (Carina Istra, "Trente-cinq ans, le bel âge pour le Chêne Noir," *La Provence*, Sep. 25, 2002).
14. "Le Living Theatre est devenu, à la faveur des événements de mai, le symbole du Festival d'Avignon 1968" (Edith Rappaport, "*Paradise Now:* Un cataclysme théâtral," *France nouvelle*, July 31, 1968).
15. Gelas, *Théâtre*, 30.
16. "leur faire comprendre que le festival ne peut se dérouler comme si Mai 68 n'avait pas dressé ses barricades" (Alfred Simon, "Le festival des enragés," *Esprit*, no. 375, November 1968), 552.
17. Quoted in Bardot, *Jean Vilar*, 504.
18. "les Avignonnais ont cru voir arriver des suppôts de Satan" (Guy Dumur, "Satan à Avignon" [Satan in Avignon], *Le nouvel observateur*, July 22–28, 1968).
19. Judith Malina, interview by author, New York City, May 22, 2004.
20. John Tytell, *The Living Theatre: Art, Exile, and Outrage* (New York: Grove Press, 1995), 226.
21. Ibid.

22. Collective Creation of the Living Theatre, written down by Judith Malina and Julian Beck, in *Paradise Now* (New York: Vintage Books, 1971), 5.

23. Aldo Rostagno, with Julian Beck and Judith Malina, *We, the Living Theatre* (New York: Ballantine, 1970), 172–73.

24. Collective Creation of the Living Theatre, 140.

25. "Le Living théâtre est fou, mais quel théâtre! Et quel document sur l'époque" (Réjane Tronel, "Aux Carmes d'Avignon 'Paradise Now' par le 'Living Theatre'" (*Le dauphine libéré,* July 23, 1968).

26. "Le festival d'Avignon est mort" (Claude Baignères, quoted in "Après le Meridional, la presse française indignée par le 'Living Theater,'" *Le Meridional,* July 27, 1968).

27. Duffaut, quoted in *Le Marseillaise,* July 28, 1968.

28. Rostagno, Beck, and Malina, *We, the Living Theatre,* 222.

29. Malina, interview.

30. "Pendant la révolution française, entre 89 et 95, les théâtres ont joué tous les soirs, après tout" (quoted in Réjane Tronel, "Jean Vilar: Les manifestations d'Avignon, une caricature dérisoire des événements de Paris en mai," *Le dauphine libéré,* Aug. 6, 1968).

31. "Avec 'Paradise Now' (comme pour les événements de mai), 'le théâtre en est arrivé au point où it faut que les choses crèvent pour repartir et recommencer.' Tout est rasé: acteurs, spectateurs sont remise en question. Plus de pièce écrite, de rôle, de salle ni de scène. La notion de spectacle même est menacée" (Rappaport, "*Paradise Now:* Un cataclysme théâtral," 12).

32. "la situation était extrêmement complexe, confuse, Avignon était une marmite bouillante où un gigantesque psychodrame se donnait. Son but, sa fonction, exorciser Mai 68, à droite et à gauche" (Gelas, *Théâtre,* 38–39).

33. "Pour la première fois à Avignon, le spectacle n'est plus seulement sur scène, il est partout, dans la rue, dans l'ombre de la mairie, de la préfecture, des commissariats. La pièce est politique. Elle s'appelle: 'Dans le jungle d'Avignon ou le festival de la peur.' Tout le monde la joue" (Maurel, "Notre époque").

Iterations of Conscience

in Performance

The Catonsville Nine, Their Protest,
Their Trial, and Their Docudramas

Jim Stacy

O_N M_{AY} 17, 1968, with protests against the Vietnam War growing louder across the United States, seven men and two women entered a draft board office in the Knights of Columbus Hall in Catonsville, Maryland, and carted away 378 draft files in wire baskets. With an invited TV cameraman capturing the action, they took the baskets to an open field and burned the files with ten pounds of homemade napalm, using a recipe lifted from a Green Beret training manual (two parts gasoline to one part Ivory soap flakes). Each had a hand in making the napalm, and each threw at least one match onto the already flaming files. As the papers burned, a few of the protesters articulated their beliefs, commented on the nature of that day's action, and prayed together as they awaited their arrest. Onlookers did not see the image of the typical on-campus protester, no long-haired hippies in faded, torn blue jeans and T-shirts declaring, "Make love, not war." In fact, three of the men wore coats and ties, and three wore coats and clerical collars. The two women wore skirts and blouses. Their hairstyles were conservative. All were ardent Catholic activists, including three priests.

When the police arrived, the television camera captured the arrest. An officer counted each protester as they were loaded into the paddy wagon, giving the media a new story with new media heroes (or villains): "the Catonsville Nine." That day an already-prepared news release explained their motivation: "We destroy these draft records not only because they exploit our young men but because they represent misplaced power concentrated in the ruling class of America. . . . We confront the Catholic church, other Christian bodies and the synagogues of America with their silence and cowardice in the face of our country's crimes." As a result of the confrontation the protesters faced charges ranging from damaging government property and conspiracy to assault (in taking the files, they had inadvertently scratched an employee).[1]

The actual destruction of the files accomplished very little, for the Selective Service office was able to reassemble the files and continue its conscriptions. However, the protesters had other goals in mind. First, they were creating a symbolic protest, its components carefully calculated, and they made sure the media were present so that an audience of millions would see the news reports throughout the world. With the assassination of John Kennedy the nation had learned the power of the still-young medium, television, to communicate to the nation the actualities of live events in ways that have great visceral impact on a mass audience. Television offered direct access to the public psyche. During the Vietnam War era the government and the protesters learned how to use that medium to depict their versions of reality and to create events accordingly. Nowadays, it is commonplace to see manipulation of the media by politicians, by businesses, by celebrities, and by terrorists. Without media coverage 9/11 would have been only a tragic event; with media coverage it was an "event performance," with Osama Bin Laden as its producer and the world as its audience. Even the current war in Iraq can be viewed as a surreal series of event performances, according to Robin Andersen, a "made-for-TV war merg[ing] news with cinematic references and reality-show camera angles"[2]—and photo ops. Richard Schechner and other performance theorists have made it quite clear that events can be performed and that "actuals" can be as much a part of *performance* as can fictions.[3] In examining the relationship between theatre and propaganda, we can see how the Catonsville protest generated an interesting succession of *performances*—from the actual events of the file burning and the subsequent trial (both preplanned, to some extent scripted, and witnessed) to its aesthetic manifestations onstage and onscreen. By elevating history to dramatic art, Daniel Berrigan, one of the priest protesters and author of *The Trial of the Catonsville Nine,* found a way to keep alive the consciences of the Nine, speaking not only to the world of the Vietnam War era but also to the world of any war era, our own included.

The Trial

In going beyond the initial protest and their demonstration of moral commitment, the Catonsville Nine pursued an even more significant goal: a deliberate legal confrontation, opening the opportunity for another event performance, a trial. From October 5 to October 9, 1968, they were given the opportunity in open court to present details of their lives as testimony to the sincerity behind their actions and to articulate their motivating beliefs. John and Rosemary Bannan point out that the Catonsville Nine were among the first peace militants to "prompt arrest by deliberately breaking the law and using their trials as forums in which to challenge both the morality and legality of the government's military policy," thus following in the traditions of other moral heroes such as Socrates and Jesus.[4] Having virtually no power as protesters on the street to influence government policy, they sought the support of an institution that did have influential power: the American legal system. "By acting heroically, they established a situation in which a federal judge and jury could also act heroically," Karen Malpede Taylor writes.[5]

To their deep disappointment, the judge instructed the jury that conscience was not a matter to be considered in a court of law. The jury returned with verdicts of guilty, and the defendants received sentences from two to three and a half years. Two of the Nine, Thomas Lewis and Philip Berrigan, had already been convicted for participating in the event performance staged by the Baltimore Four a year earlier.[6] At the time of the protest action at Catonsville, they were out on bond pending an appeal; at the time of the Catonsville trial they had lost that appeal and were serving that sentence in federal prison. After the conviction of the Nine the defendants were free on bond for some sixteen months with an appeal to the Supreme Court, which refused to hear the case. The Berrigan brothers and two others went into hiding but were eventually caught and served their sentences, with Mary Molan staying "underground" for nine years before surrendering.

The Play: Critical Reaction

Remarkably, the event performances at the Catonsville draft office and later in the courtroom inspired additional iterations, three docudramas that would guarantee wider and future audiences: a play script by Daniel Berrigan (*The Trial of the Catonsville Nine*, first published in 1971 and revised in 2004),[7] a movie version of the play (1972), and a recent documentary film by Lynne Sachs (*Investigation of a Flame*, 2001). Working with more than twelve hundred pages of actual transcripts of the trial in the summer of 1969, Berrigan says, "somewhat in the manner of the new 'factual theatre,'" he hoped to "induce out of the density of the matter an art form worthy of the passionate acts and words of the Nine."[8] He also writes that the work had only one purpose: "to wind the spring tighter."[9] Berrigan's work was first performed at the Mark Taper Forum in Los Angeles in August 1971 under the direction of Gordon Davidson. While Berrigan was in prison, a script was prepared by Saul Levitt for presentation Off-Broadway, using the priest's published text. The play was later transferred to Broadway (where it earned Davidson a "Best Director" Tony nomination in 1972).

Reviewing the production at a time prior to the articulation of postmodern performance theory, many critics nonetheless recognized that *Catonsville Nine* is more than a conventional play. They claimed the original action was an example of protest as theatre; it had a constructed plot and actors who were performing not for themselves but for a television audience. The trial became the second act of a performance piece. Berrigan's play script merely extends the words and actions of the Nine to additional audiences, who can appreciate anew their ideas and their courage. Stanley Kaufmann claimed that "the event itself was a drama, and . . . what we are seeing is simply its natural continuum, its destiny."[10] Taking a similar perspective, Clive Barnes said, "The play is not derived from the action, but inherent in the action, for it is a single political protest, first made flesh and now made legend."[11] Other critics wrote similarly: "It is more document than documentary, more personal testimony than play"; it was "a radiant explication of the Gospels . . . , a sermon, an exhortation to action, but it was not a play"; and "this 'play' exists and exerts power as the stage embodiment of a reality rather than as artistic imitation of reality."[12] Concurring with this final point of view, Walter Kerr contended that the viewer did not watch the stage principals as performing actors but as "emissaries" for the real principals, who could not speak for themselves because they were in prison. "We attend wholly to the words we know to be Berrigan's, straining our ears not for an actor's inflection but for what may prove to be a prophet's voice," Kerr wrote.[13] More than thirty years after the fact, the newly published script of the play is both a document of war protest and a work of performance literature. As a traditional play it lacks unexpected developments and character growth—those hooks of the well-made play designed to capture audience interest. The impact of the piece is actual, not metaphoric; actual events are enriched by aesthetic selection just as the aesthetic is enriched by the power of a real act of civil disobedience. Such is the power of the documentary drama: fact, art, and performance serving one another for maximum impact (most evident recently in the success of *The Laramie Project* by Moises Kaufman and the Tectonic Theater Project).

For many New York critics the passion and power of the production were unquestionable. Harold Clurman claimed that *Catonsville Nine*

was "an absorbing event of sobering impact," and Marilyn Stasio said
it had "the factual honesty of documentary and the emotional impact
of a Greek tragedy."[14] John Simon, known for his acerbic tongue, was
moved to write of *Catonsville Nine:* "During the presentation, I was
constantly fighting back my tears—not out of shame, only so as not to
miss anything that was being said on stage. Afterward, for a long time,
I could not, and did not care to, speak. Now I scarcely know how to
write about the playwright and his eight co-defendants—how to criticize them. I would like simply to canonize them." In exploring the
theme, Simon said Berrigan was dealing with "the ancient dilemma:
expediency versus justice. . . . The issue at stake is even greater than war
or peace, enormous as that issue is. It is human nobility, imagination,
vision up against human blindness, bureaucratic legality, and legalized
butchery."[15] Ned O'Gorman contended that the defendants were cor-
rect in their readings of the times and that the play successfully reports
their perceptions: "the war *is* evil; the death of the innocent *does* increase; American guilt *is* clear; the silence of the churches and the government *is* shameful and vile, for in the face of the massacre they still
are morally indolent."[16]

The Play: Testimonies

In terms of plot the play is structured linearly as a trial, beginning
with jury selection (in which the defense refused to take part) and ending with a guilty verdict, a known historical outcome. Thus, playwright
Berrigan puts the focus on the "characters" of the play whose trial testimonies are edited to sound anew the personal stories of the Nine,
their moral philosophies, and the poetry of their ideas (written in the
script in free verse format). In the play the Catonsville Nine include
Daniel Berrigan, a Jesuit priest and poet; Philip Berrigan, a Josephite
priest, activist, and World War II veteran; Thomas Lewis, an artist; John
Hogan, a carpenter and former Maryknoll brother; Marjorie and Thomas
Melville, a former nun and priest, married to each other; George Mische,
a youth worker; Mary Moylan, a nurse; and David Darst, a brilliant Harvard scholar. They spend much of the early part of the trial relating
their backgrounds and exploring their motivations for acting at Catonsville. As revealed in their trial testimony, while their experiences vary,
all of the Nine come to see how the United States misused its military
might around the world (in Vietnam, Uganda, and several Central
American countries, most notably Guatemala). With their moral indig-
nation aroused, each is drawn magnetically to the opportunity to make
a bold statement at Catonsville. In the introduction to the newly pub-

lished version of the play script, Daniel Berrigan writes of his own decision-making process:

> We improvised our lives as we went along. To be sure, we had certain insights, having to do with community and nonviolence. We had come upon them in the course of a long loneliness, a long exposure, a long defeat, as conditions worsened around us, and the light sank lower. But we could be reasonably sure of one thing, in the midst of great and general perplexity. That is to say, we had not sleepwalked toward Catonsville, nor toward the trials that followed. We went into court as we had gone into the draft center—wide awake, neither insane nor amnesiac.[17]

In the play the Berrigan brothers serve as bookends for the largest section of the piece, "The Day of the Nine Defendants," with Philip speaking first and Daniel last. The first priest in America to be tried and convicted for a political crime, Philip Berrigan, who died in 2002, spent some eleven years in prison over a span of thirty-two years for numerous illegal event performances of conscience and resistance. Philip recalls in court the early life of Daniel, himself, and their other four brothers in a poverty-stricken home in Minnesota and their disciplinarian schooling at a Catholic school two miles away. During World War II Philip was a decorated officer, a second lieutenant in the infantry, and an "enthusiastic participant" in the Allies' cause. After the war he entered the Society of St. Joseph to become a priest and worked to better the conditions of African Americans in the early civil rights movement, which he links directly to his decision to act at Catonsville. Citing the heritage of civil disobedience in this country, Philip recalls his early involvement in the peace movement and his earlier event performance at the Baltimore draft board office, where blood was poured on military records.[18]

One especially relevant experience for Daniel Berrigan was his trip in 1968 to Hanoi, North Vietnam, to accompany home three American prisoners. While there, he survived an American bombing attack and also witnessed the deaths of innocent civilians by U.S. planes. Also weighing on his final decision to act at Catonsville was the self-immolation of a high school student in Syracuse, New York, in the spring of 1968. After setting himself on fire, the dying youth suffered for a month in a hospital, where Daniel visited him. It was a horrifying scene and a powerful reminder of the atrocities he had witnessed in Vietnam, "the Land of Burning Children." Berrigan testifies:

> So I went to Catonsville and burned some papers because the burning of children is inhuman and unbearable. I went to Catonsville because I had

gone to Hanoi. I went to Catonsville because my brother was a man and I must be a man, and because I knew at length I could not announce the gospel from a pedestal. I must act as a Christian sharing the risks and burdens and anguish of those whose lives were placed in the breach by us. (92)

In addition to sharing life experiences, each defendant is given the opportunity to express his or her moral beliefs. Their words are often passionate and incisive, raising issues that are uncomfortable and even painful for the judge and jury to face. For example, in answering the judge's insistence that the defendants stop talking so much about seemingly irrelevant background, such as Thomas Melville's experiences in Guatemala, Melville says, "Eighty-five percent of the people in Guatemala live in misery. You don't live in misery; perhaps that is why you don't worry about it" (56).

Mary Moylan passionately expresses her horror at the thought of using napalm on people: "As a nurse my profession is to preserve life, to prevent disease. To a nurse the effect of napalm on human beings is apparent. I think of children and women bombed by napalm, burned alive by a substance which does not roll off. It is a jelly; it adheres; it continues burning" (65). To her, the action of burning the draft files was a declaration of her wish to celebrate life as a true Christian.

Thomas Lewis claims that their intent was to save lives:

I wasn't concerned with the law. I wasn't even thinking about the law. I was thinking of what those records meant. . . . I was concerned with the lives of innocent people. I went in there with the intent of stopping what the files justify. The young men whose files we destroyed have not yet been drafted, may not be drafted, may not be sent to Vietnam for cannon fodder. My intent in going there was to save lives.

The judge asks Lewis if it occurred to him that other men would be sent in the place of those on file in Catonsville. Lewis replies, "Buy why, Your Honor? Why this? Why does it have to be like this? You are accepting the fact that if these men are not sent other men will be sent. You are not even asking what can be done to stop the insane killing, what can be done to stop the genocide. . . . You are accepting this as in Nazi Germany people accepted the massacre of other people" (48).

The Berrigan brothers offer their own passionate and eloquent testimony, such as when Philip pleads before the court:

The real issue is: how can men serve love and war? The fact is, they can't. Most Americans have great difficulty seeing the I, the self, as being, the we, humanity. . . . We think we can rape a people and have them love us. We cannot ravage the ecology of Indochina, kill ten civilians for every soldier, and expect anything but do-or-die opposition. We cannot fight the abstraction of Communism by killing the people who believe in it. We cannot talk peace while our deeds give the lie to our words. We can't have it both ways. (33, Samuel French)[19]

Philip seeks a nonviolent revolution in the world in the way of the Gospels or Gandhi. American institutions as they now exist are incapable of making such a change; they have lost contact with the people. The sad question facing America, Philip suggests, is, "How much time is left this country, this magnificent, frantic, insane, nation-empire to which God has entrusted so much of the future of mankind?" (48, Samuel French). The defense attorney asks Daniel Berrigan to read from a meditation he wrote just before the protest:

We say: killing is disorder; life and gentleness and community and unselfishness is the only order we recognize. For the sake of that order we risk our liberty, our good name. The time is past when good men can remain silent, when obedience can segregate men from public risk, when the poor can die without defense. How many indeed must die before our voices are heard; how many must be tortured, dislocated, starved, maddened? How long must the world's resources be raped in service of legalized murder? When at what point will you say no to this war? (94)

He sees a nation in which Christians pay more homage to Caesar and Mars than to Christ. But in draft resisters, civil rights activists, and war protesters he sees a source of inspiration for the Nine: "We think of such men and women in the world, in our nation, in the churches, and the stone in our breast is dissolved and we take heart once more" (95).

The Play: The Verdict

In addition to the defendants, Berrigan's play gives voice to the judge, the defense attorney, the prosecutor, and one witness (the clerk from the draft board office). All are unnamed in the play script, their courtroom roles serving instead to identify them. None of them speaks in the free verse form used by Berrigan for the defendants' testimonies in the new version of the script. The prosecutor is relentless in his objections to the testimony of the defendants about their background motivations for their protest. In his closing argument the prosecutor reminds the jury that they are to decide the legality of the defendants' action, not the legality of the Vietnam War. He admits that the defendants are reasonable in thinking that the war is immoral and illegal; it is a defensible stance. "But our problems are not going to be solved by people who deliberately violate our laws, the foundation and support for an ordered and just and civilized society," he asserts (101).

Having persevered with his clients throughout the objections by the prosecution, the defense attorney admits in his closing arguments that this case has become one of intense personal involvement for him. "For myself, I must confess with more pride than I could adequately describe, I have come to love and respect the men and women who stand before the court," he says (102). He then reminds the court that this case need not be one that narrowly decides the legality of a specific action. "The trial of Socrates was not merely a question of a man sowing confusion and distrust among the youth of Athens; the trial of Jesus could not be reduced to one of conspiracy against the empire," he tells the jury (103). The defense contends that the draft office was an agent of violence; its files were death certificates. Thus, the defendants were striking at a vital link in the war machine in an effort to stop the illegal, immoral killing. The defendants, along with thousands of other protesters, had tried to end the war with "words, writings, marching, fasting, demonstrating," but they "have failed to change a single American decision in Vietnam; failed even momentarily to slow the unnatural, senseless destruction of men, women and children, including the destruction of our own sons—a destruction wrought in the name of a policy that passes all human understanding," the lawyer pleads (105–6). Finally he calls the jurors to be guided by their reason and conscience.

The judge is put into the disturbing position of contradicting the defense attorney: "The jury may not decide this case on the basis of conscience. The jury will decide this case solely on the basis of the facts presented in this courtroom by both sides" (105). The judge in the actual trial, Roszel Thomsen, cried as he handed down the sentence. The judge in the play does not break down, but the script does portray some of his anguish. The judge is pressed to admit, "As a man, I would be a very funny sort if I were not moved by your sincerity on the stand . . . and by your views." He even agrees with the defendants' position on the war: "We can never accomplish what we would like to accomplish, or give a better life to people, if we are going to keep spending so much money for war" (115). But he is willing to wait and let the institutions of government slowly respond to the will of the people. Finally, he will not yield his legalistic position: "Good character is not a defense for breaking the law." Echoing Robert Bolt's Sir Thomas More, he adds, "I am not God almighty. I did what the law required me to do. All we can do is our best" (117). He sadly accepts the unbending opposition of the defendants, who ask that the discussion be ended because they realize they are making no headway but only seem to be looking for mercy or compromise. "We do not wish that primary blade of contention to be honed down to no edge at all by a gentleman's agreement, whereby you agree with us and we with you. We do not agree with you, and we thank you," Daniel Berrigan tells the judge (119). As their ethical discussion reaches an impasse, Daniel asks the judge if the court will allow a recitation of "The Lord's Prayer." Harvey Cox, a Harvard Divinity School professor who was present at the trial, describes the prayer as "a Pentecostal Moment" in the courtroom as "women sobbed, United States marshals bowed their heads and wiped their eyes. . . . City police, bearded peace workers, nuns and court stenographers prayed together: 'For thine is the Kingdom and the Power and the Glory.'"[20] When the jury returns its verdict of guilty, Daniel Berrigan again thanks the judge and the prosecutor before concluding, "We agree that this is the greatest day of our lives" (122). They were guilty of a moral victory.

On the Screen

In 1972 actor Gregory Peck produced the film version of the play, *The Trial of the Catonsville Nine,* again directed by Gordon Davidson in a straightforward transference of the script to the screen—yet another iteration.[21] In the film the characters literally become larger than life, and close-ups serve to enhance the nonverbal communication of the fervent commitment of the Nine to their spoken ideals; the eyes of the actors are appropriately lit with unshakeable integrity and zealous belief. Thus, with the movie the original event finds yet another outlet for the expression of conscience. Although the film did not enjoy mainstream distribution or box office success, millions more have seen it in art houses and film festivals over the last three decades.

In 2001, almost thirty years after the making of the movie, documentary filmmaker Lynne Sachs revisited the event performances, taking a poetic approach with her *Investigation of a Flame,* filling it not only with interviews of the surviving Catonsville Nine and "supporting case" but also with images of flowers, Vietnamese peasants, American combat soldiers, war protesters, flag-draped caskets, and politicians.[22] Espousing the then-current "Domino Theory" (if Vietnam falls to the communists, so will the rest of Asia), LBJ is shown further declaring to Congress and his television audience that the freedom of U.S. citizens is at stake in Vietnam. (Johnson's hyperbolic justification seems false and hollow in light of the startling revelations of former Secretary of Defense Robert McNamara in another documentary film, Errol Morris's *The Fog of War.*)

The interviews with seven of the protesters, thirty-two years after the deed, resonate with the very real humanity of ordinary people who did extraordinary things. Tom Lewis cites the early draft-card burnings as inspiration for the Catonsville action. Philip Berrigan compares blood and fire as symbols at the core of his protest events. Daniel Berrigan recalls when his brother visited him at Cornell to invite his participation in the Catonsville action, "whereupon I begin to quake in my boots." But after much soul searching Daniel decided, "I didn't want to do it, but I couldn't not do it." Much of what the protesters contribute to *Investigation of a Flame* is a reflection of their trial testimony, enhanced in the film by the visual images of moral heroes aged by thirty-two more years of living.

Sachs makes powerful use of interviews with three others involved in the trial, Steve Sachs (no relation to Lynne), the prosecutor; Mary Murphy, the draft board office clerk; and one of the jurors. Although he has acknowledged his own opposition to the war in Vietnam, the prosecutor viewed the action of the Catonsville Nine as "excessive and arrogant," explaining, "You don't burn what you hate." He eloquently quotes from Robert Bolt's *A Man for All Seasons* the famous lines of Thomas More about the rule of law:

> MORE: The law, Roper, the law. I know what's legal not what's right. And I'll stick to what's legal.
> ROPER: Then you set man's law above God's!
> MORE: No, far below; but let me draw your attention to a fact—I'm not God. The currents and eddies of right and wrong, which you find such plain sailing, I can't navigate. I'm no voyager. But in the thickets of the law, oh, there I'm a forester. I doubt if there's a man alive who could follow me there, thank God.[23]

We see the office clerk in black and white footage from 1968 immediately after the incident and, looking much older, thirty-two years later, as she reflects, "I don't know whether it was right or wrong or why or who or what. We just tried to help out . . . to make our boys as safe as we could and send them people to help them when we could." Her seeming need, shaded with doubt, to justify her role in the draft and the war elicits sympathy, as does the juror who chokes up on the verge of tears when she expresses her admiration for the people whom she voted to convict: "I could never be that courageous."

In a recent telephone interview Lynne Sachs said that Daniel Berrigan and the other protesters readily acknowledged that they carefully planned their protest as "a symbolic art piece," designed for the widest publicity possible.[24] The protesters chose clothing that would identify them with "the heartland of America," not with any radical elements or hippie peaceniks. Sachs also confirms that the protesters notified the press of their plans in advance so that a newspaper photographer, a television cameraman, and a sound man would be on hand as the files burned. She said that one reporter was initially accused of being an accomplice, and authorities tried unsuccessfully to confiscate his TV tape, which was then secreted away for over thirty years until it was given to Sachs to make the documentary.

Over the course of more than three decades the Catonsville Nine have expressed their consciences to the world, first in an act of civil disobedience, an "event performance," in which they risked their reputations, security, and freedom. Their trial gave them a further opportunity to sound their beliefs so that their eloquent whispers could momentarily drown out the guns and bombs of their government. The guilty verdict could have ended the matter and left the Nine as a footnote in a history book. But in transferring the trial to the stage, Berrigan has converted history into art, assuring himself and his codefendants an ongoing present tense for their beliefs. The court records will show the particulars of their testimony; performers of Berrigan's dramatic poem will keep the event alive and in the present tense of performance. As part of the typography of the free-verse testimony of the defendants, Berrigan opted to use no periods at the ends of sentences, perhaps from the conviction that the inspirational ideas contained within should not stop, even in deference to punctuation. Robin Andersen, professor of communications and media studies at Fordham University, writes in the preface to the 2004 edition of the play: "*The Trial of the Catonsville Nine* is part of a culture of resistance and wisdom though rarely openly celebrated. . . . [The Berrigans'] spirit of hope and resistance is a living collective memory, one that challenges and threatens the makers of war and its weapons. It is time to bring that unconscious memory back into the open and celebrate the power of these words."[25] Andersen also offers in an afterword a compelling application of the issues and the ideals of the Catonsville event performances and their texts to the current fighting and dying in Iraq, Afghanistan, and elsewhere.[26] As terror and war continue to march through the new millennium, the words of the Catonsville Nine deserve to be sounded and heard again and again until some final punctuation for war can be found.

Notes

1. See Murray Polner and Jim O'Grady, *Disarmed and Dangerous: The Radical Lives and Times of Daniel and Philip Berrigan* (New York: Basic Books, 1997). For details on Catonsville and other Vietnam War protests by the Berrigans see chapters 8–12. Numerous other sources on Catholic activism and the

Vietnam War protest movement corroborate and add details to the account of the Catonsville event, including actual footage from *Investigation of a Flame,* a documentary film written and directed by Lynne Sachs (Brooklyn: First Run Icarus Films, 2001).

2. Robin Andersen, second afterword, in Daniel Berrigan, *The Trial of the Catonsville Nine* (New York: Fordham University Press, 2004), 133.

3. Richard Schechner, "Actuals: A Look into Performance Theory," *Essays on Performance Theory, 1970–1976* (New York: Drama Book Specialists, 1977), 3–35.

4. John F. Bannan and Rosemary S. Bannan, *Law, Morality, and Vietnam: The Peace Militants and the Courts* (Bloomington: Indiana University Press, 1974), 3–4.

5. Karen Malpede Taylor, *People's Theatre in America* (New York: Drama Book Specialists, 1972), 280.

6. In 1967 Philip Berrigan, Thomas Lewis, and two other men (dubbed "the Baltimore Four") entered the Baltimore draft board office and poured blood (a mixture of their own and duck's blood) over some of the Selective Service records. Thirteen years later he and seven other activists (the "Plowshares Eight") entered a General Electric nuclear missile facility and staged a dramatic event performance. They poured blood (their own) on nose cones intended for Mark 12A nuclear warheads and also hammered on them, following up on the biblical call by Isaiah to "beat swords into plowshares," inspiring dozens of "Plowshares" event performances since then. For more details on these event performances see Polner and O'Grady, *Disarmed and Dangerous;* Arthur L. Laffin and Anne Montgomery, eds., *Swords into Plowshares: Nonviolent Direct Action for Disarmament* (San Francisco: Harper and Row, 1987); and Fred A. Wilcox, *Uncommon Martyrs: The Plowshares Movement and the Catholic Left* (Reading, MA: Addison-Wesley, 1991).

7. Daniel Berrigan's *The Trial of the Catonsville Nine* was originally published in 1971 by Samuel French and included a cowriter credit for Saul Levitt. The new and revised edition (with Berrigan credited as the sole author) was published by Fordham University Press in 2004. The revisions include the structuring of the script by days of the trial ("The Day of the Jury of Peers," "The Day of the Facts of the Case," "The Day of the Nine Defendants," "The Day of Summation," and "The Day of Verdict"), editing of some of the previously included testimony, and a typographic arrangement that presents the defendants' testimony as free verse, without punctuation.

8. Quoted in Taylor, *People's Theatre in America,* 280.

9. Berrigan, introduction to *The Trial of the Catonsville Nine* (New York: Fordham University Press, 2004), xviii.

10. Stanley Kaufman, review of *The Trial of the Catonsville Nine, New Republic,* March 6, 1971, 29.

11. Clive Barnes, "Theatre: Riveting Work by Berrigan," *New York Times,* Feb. 8, 1971.

12. Catharine Hughes, *Plays, Politics, and Polemics* (New York: Drama Book Specialists, 1973), 83; Ned O'Gorman, "Berrigan, the Church, and the 'Nine,'"

New York Times, May 30, 1971; and Martin Gottfried, "'The Trial of the Caton-sville Nine' . . . Powerful and Inspiring," *Women's Wear Daily,* Feb. 9, 1971, 35.

13. Walter Kerr, "Their 'J'Accuse' Is Chilling," *New York Times,* Feb. 14, 1971.

14. Harold Clurman, "Theatre Review," *Nation,* Feb. 22, 1971, 254; Marilyn Stasio, review of *The Trial of the Catonsville Nine, Cue,* Feb. 15, 1971, 15.

15. John Simon, "Saints for Our Times," *New York,* Feb. 22, 1971, 66.

16. O'Gorman, "Berrigan, the Church, and the 'Nine.'"

17. Berrigan, introduction, xx.

18. See Berrigan, *Trial of the Catonsville Nine,* 21–31. Subsequent references to script quotations are from the Fordham edition of the play and are identified parenthetically in the text by page number only. The two quotations from the original Samuel French version are marked as "Samuel French."

19. The omission of this passionate expression in the Fordham edition is puzzling, especially in light of its contemporary relevance.

20. Harvey Cox Jr., "Tongues of Fire: *The Trial of the Catonsville Nine,*" in *The Witness of the Berrigans,* ed. Stephen Halpert and Tom Murray (New York: Doubleday, 1972), 22–23.

21. *The Trial of the Catonsville Nine,* feature film, directed by Gordon Davidson, produced by Gregory Peck, screenplay by Daniel Berrigan and Saul Levitt (Melville Productions, 1972).

22. *Investigation of a Flame,* documentary film, directed and written by Lynne Sachs (Brooklyn: First Run Icarus Films, 2001).

23. Quoted in the documentary by prosecutor Steve Sachs (originally from Robert Bolt's play *A Man for All Seasons*).

24. Lynne Sachs, telephone interview by the author, Feb. 21, 2005.

25. Andersen, preface to *The Trial of the Catonsville Nine* (New York: Fordham University Press, 2004), xvi.

26. See Andersen, second afterword, 129–42.

Where Have All the Protestors Gone?

1960s Radical Theatre and Contemporary Theatrical Responses to U.S. Military Involvement in Iraq

David Callaghan

As AMERICA'S INVOLVEMENT in Vietnam escalated during the 1950s and 1960s, both Hollywood and the American theatre faced the question of how they would represent the war. A few films emerged as early as the 1950s that depicted a "Western" struggle—first French and then American—against communist expansion in Southeast Asia. With the exception of John Wayne's controversially received *The Green Berets* in 1967, however, the film industry did not portray combat situations in Vietnam throughout the duration of the conflict.[1] Rather, it concentrated its efforts on war-related topics such as antiwar protests or "alienated" returning Vietnam veterans. Thus, it was not until the 1980s that a steady flow of mainstream films depicting an American presence in Vietnam was produced in Hollywood.

In contrast, much of the emerging avant-garde theatre community quickly engaged and frequently criticized the U.S. military presence in Vietnam. In his detailed study of the theatre of this period, *Levitating the Pentagon*, J. W. Fenn characterizes this work as "radical" in contrast to less politically motivated "experimental" groups such as the Open Theater. The main purpose of the work of radical groups was "the dissemination of message rather than experimentation with nuance of medium," with that message typically including distinct "antiwar goals."[2] The period of the 1960s in America, and elsewhere, resulted in numerous radical political movements and the challenging of institutional authority and value systems. Much of this protest eventually coalesced around the Vietnam War as a symbol of "establishment" corruption and misguided policy. Other areas of counterculture protest, such as the media-labeled "hippie" movement, advocated the formation of alternative lifestyles and cultures (communal living, for example) in lieu of overhauling, or overthrowing, the existing system. In his 1971 essay "Growing Out of the Sixties," Richard Gilman labeled the dominant 1960s theatrical current as "politicized and placed in the service of a radicalism that sought to affiliate itself with the broader radicalism outside," not to mention a tendency toward using theatre as a "means of redemption."[3] Many years later the United States is once again at war; and, as in the 1960s, various theatre companies have begun to engage our policies in various forms. Although there has been a range of recent theatrical response to American military involvement overseas since 9/11, particularly in Iraq, I argue that such work has been much less oppositional or even critical of U.S. policy than the radical theatre movements that overtly resisted our involvement in Vietnam. The reasons for that change, of course, are rooted in a complex web of cultural, economic, and aesthetic factors that have influenced production of new plays, as well as audience reception of that work over the last thirty years.

The U.S. sociopolitical landscape changed very quickly during the 1970s, after American troops began to withdraw from Vietnam, which arguably precipitated a surprisingly quick collapse of an antiwar movement that had been increasingly weakened by in-fighting and a growing willingness to use violent tactics in some circles. As Todd Gitlin noted in his seminal study *The Sixties: Years of Hope, Days of Rage,* "by the early Seventies the upheaval was over—as mysteriously as it had appeared, and as worldwide. . . . 'The Sixties' receded into haze and myth."[4] The radical theatre community was not exempt from the disillusionment and fragmentation that generally characterized the counterculture of the late 1960s and early 1970s. Judith Malina, who cofounded the Living Theatre with Julian Beck in 1947, commented on this shift after the infamous radical company returned from Europe in 1968 to present four new collectively created political theatre pieces, most notably *Paradise Now.* Malina lamented that "six months ago our intention was to radicalize our audiences. This is no longer our intention. We are facing audiences that are already radicalized. . . . [H]ere, we're surrounded by another political milieu."[5] Their desire to find "the next question" in relation to theatre and politics in part drove the Living Theatre to abandon playing in conventional spaces by 1970, as the company felt increasingly out-of-touch with the growing violent nature of some sectors of radical politics and antiwar opposition (such as the street protests they encountered while playing in Berkeley). Given our more recent generally apolitical cultural and theatrical landscape, the political activism of the 1960s era, including direct opposition to the Vietnam War, often seems very distant, a quaint subject only worthy of historical inquiry and nostalgia.

Indeed, a backlash of sorts against the 1960s seemed to occur very quickly in American society, fueled perhaps by a cultural need to achieve a distance from the turmoil and divisiveness of the period. The outward-looking altruism of the 1960s counterculture imploded as the baby boomer youth culture began to grow up, make money, and focus on domestic and personal fulfillment during the "Me Decade" of the 1970s. Furthermore, the country seemed to be suffering from what former president Richard Nixon called a post-Vietnam "malaise" of sorts,[6] with economists and political conservatives lamenting rising unemployment, urban crime and the potential "collapse" of American cities, postwar debt, gas shortages, a hostage crisis in Iran, and an ongoing difficult period of "coming to terms" with the impact of the war on returning American troops and the social fabric of our nation. As a recent *New York Times* article entitled "Were the Good Old Days That Good?" observed, domestic U.S. productivity and income levels rose steadily after World War II, until 1973, followed by a "horrific slowdown" that lasted until the 1990s, when productivity fell to an annual growth rate of less than 1.5 percent and median income stagnated.[7] Middle-class angst and a growing loss of faith in American institutions were reflected in the menacing urban landscape depicted in popular vigilante films such as *Dirty Harry* and *Death Wish*, where frustrated cops and citizens turned to violence outside "the system" to protect themselves and others as a kind of last-ditch effort to protect traditional American liberties.

Simultaneously, the momentum of the avant-garde and radical theatre scene also changed drastically, with major theatre journals such as *Performing Arts Journal* (PAJ) cataloging the collapse, failure, or transformation of various experimental companies. Richard Schechner, a former editor of the *Drama Review* (TDR) and the founder of the experimental ensemble the Performance Group during the 1960s, penned the most provocative and perhaps well known of these introspective pieces. Entitled "The Decline and Fall of the (American) Avant-Garde," it charged that political content disappeared from the experimental theatre community almost overnight. Schechner cited causes such as a decline in subsidies for experimental companies, the collapse of group ensembles because of interpersonal conflict, and a general lack of interest in social activism by the early 1970s.[8] Certainly the American avant-garde continued and evolved through the 1980s and 1990s, but its greater emphasis on formalism and postmodern irony seemed to increasingly marginalize the notion of an activist experimental theatre scene. Philip Auslander labels postmodern culture as one that is mass-mediatized and therefore aware of its own role and potential complicity within the larger cultural apparatus. In contrast, radical theatre companies of the 1960s such as the Living Theatre saw their participation within a "commodity economy" as unacceptable. Postmodern theatre and performance artists—and, by extension, audiences—have essentially rejected these models. High-profile experimental artists of the 1980s such as the Wooster Group, Richard Foreman, and Laurie Anderson critiqued and deconstructed postmodern culture from *within*, suggesting the possibility of an avant-garde that could conceive politics and political theatre itself in more implicit or "resistant" terms.[9] In his insightful study *The Making of American Audiences,* Richard Butsch documented the rise in home entertainment options and changes in viewing habits during the 1970s and 1980s, especially in relation to such developments as VCRs and video rental companies. He argues that the concept of a television-focused audience has been criticized as passive, in opposition to traditional theatregoers and the "collective" audiences of the 1960s counterculture that were intent on "making big changes in society." Although Butsch agrees that post-1960s American audiences are less politicized and more solitary than their earlier counterparts, he also contends that such shifts in entertainment and spectator behavior have merely produced a new kind of "autonomy" and "resistance" that offers interesting potential for merger with our former notions of explicit critical response.[10] Clearly, all of these factors have impacted the way contemporary American theatre audiences have responded to the war in Iraq.

While some 1960s-era radical theatre artists such as the Bread and Puppet Theater continued to create new works that critiqued U.S. foreign policy in such places as El Salvador, or violent struggle in sites such as Bosnia, a predominantly depoliticized American theatre community seemed an inevitable reflection of the dominant conservative climate of the Reagan-Bush years. The ideology of Reagan's presidency recalled an earlier, simpler, and supposedly stronger America based on national identity myths of American invincibility and righteousness, and Reagan's politically reactionary and often jingoistic rhetoric struck a chord with many Americans disenchanted by the social problems and sagging national morale that characterized the immediate post-1960s milieu. The intersection of art and politics in the 1980s produced a series of culture wars and a reactionary backlash against the so-called hedonism and legacy of the 1960s counterculture, including cuts in the National Endowment for the Arts (NEA), which often supported artists who were considered in violation of traditional American values. So artists interested in experimenting with radical content found themselves under siege by influential conservative forces in the government and grossly out of sync with the nostalgia-addled political climate of the era. Indeed, large audiences flocked to movie theatres to see Sylvester Stallone's Rambo character revise history and crush America's enemies in Vietnam, while in the real world Reagan's administration "heated up" the cold war, and the Soviet Union became the villain *de jour* for Hollywood's blockbuster action movies. In her provocative study *Hard Bodies,* Susan Jeffords draws a parallel between the reemergence of a post-Vietnam and 1960s counterculture "hard body" national American identity and the image of Ronald Reagan as our president (and how this relationship was reflected in various films of the 1980s). Thus, "Ronald Reagan" represented a site of "national fantasy" or "became one of the ways through which many Americans felt a connection to their national identity."[11]

The 1990s witnessed yet another political reversal: the election of President Clinton and a new era of what some have labeled "liberal excesses."[12] But the American economy also produced the first major upswing since the early 1970s. With Clinton's foreign policy deemphasizing U.S. military involvement overseas and paper fortunes being made in emerging technology markets, Americans were generally still complacent and nonpoliticized. Interestingly, the Living Theatre, which had received an almost venomous critical reception after returning to America in 1984, continued to create new, politically oriented works at their converted storefront space in a marginalized, noncommercial location on East 3rd Street in New York City, as well as street theatre pieces in the 1960s-era tradition. The company's consistently negative reviews by New York theatre critics serve as a sort of cultural barometer for how their association with the radicalism and politics of the 1960s era created an immediately wary audience reception.

Representative examples include Frank Rich's mocking the company's hippie image: "The Living Theatre is now a straggly collection of indistinguishable riffraff; the troupe could be a defrocked Moonie ashram, or maybe a seedy bus-and-truck company of *Godspell* at the end of a 15-year tour";[13] or Sy Syna's review of the troupe's 1991 production of *Rules of Civility* in *Back Stage:* "It is an often enigmatic, amateurish, pretentious and somewhat smelly assault upon the audience's sensibilities and sentiments. . . . From their collective aroma, it's clear that the frequent use of soap and water is not currently part of the Living Theatre aesthetic."[14] Perhaps the overall critical reaction of the period was best expressed by the title of a 1989 article by Howard Kissel, in which Kissel scathingly attacked the remaining vestiges of the 1960s theatre "esthetic": "Isn't the Living Theatre Dead Yet?"[15]

Even *Village Voice* critic Mark Robinson's generally positive review of their 1994 revival of their seminal 1964 production of *Mysteries and Smaller Pieces* began with a discussion of his preconceptions of the group based on their wild image from the 1960s, involving "coarsely articulated politics, coerced audience participation, embarrassing sexual rituals."[16] Thus, the conservative 1980s and the liberal 1990s were decades defined mainly by material comfort and pursuits of financial profit, with the social activism and lifestyle excesses of the "age of Aquarius" criticized in the larger culture as passé, dangerous, and somewhat embarrassing in successive years. Although I agree that some of the Living Theatre's productions and stylistic devices in this period were indeed artistically flawed, it is telling to note how much the critical discourse around their work tended to ground such responses in a larger attack on a perceived, lingering 1960s radical theatre sensibility. Only twenty years had passed since the end of the Vietnam War and the numerous theatrical productions that supported that goal, but the domestic landscape was so altered by the mid-1990s that theatrical expressions of 1960s-era passion, political scope, and even outrage seemed of virtually no interest to large-scale audiences.

Thus, when a young director like Reza Abdoh began to create visceral, politically charged productions such as *Law of Remains* and *Tight, Right, White,* his worldview and aesthetic represented an anomaly in relation to the larger theatrical and even experimental scene in New York City. Indeed, Marvin Carlson noted Abdoh's generational uniqueness in his commitment to a 1960s-like, Artaudian-inspired theatre, reiterating Schechner's earlier charge that most recent experimental theatre in America had seemed "more intellectually abstract, more technological," in contrast to the highly "exhilarating theatre" of the 1960s. He also argued that Abdoh's work almost assaulted the audience through its use of multiple layers of stimuli, frequently involving a complex synthesis of actors, shifting locations, numerous and simultaneous focal points, and the use of video and film. Thus, while stylistically akin to postmodern artists such as The Wooster Group or Richard Foreman, his plays were rare in their willingness to engage a variety of overtly political social, sexual, and racial "politics and phantoms."[17]

While standing as a somewhat solitary figure during the 1990s, Abdoh's exhilarating but short-lived career as a radically oriented theatre artist serves as a sort of transition to the artistic climate of our post-9/11 world, which, as in the 1960s, has been forced to respond to seismic shifts in our geopolitical and cultural landscape. As in the Vietnam era, we now find ourselves involved in an escalating, and controversial, military conflict, with American troops stationed in Afghanistan and Iraq. Certainly the attacks on American soil on 9/11 produced an immediate and understandable patriotic groundswell of support for President Bush and provided a different context for the use of American troops overseas. We are at war under a president and cabinet that have greatly expanded the use of the American military as an instrument of foreign policy. Although there has been a substantial degree of support for such policies, based in part on rationales of combating terrorism, the war and many aspects of the president's foreign policy agenda are increasingly under scrutiny, debate, and even opposition in the media and various political circles domestically and overseas. Early in 2005 U.S. Army recruiters admitted publicly that their monthly quotas would not be met, and mainstream weeklies such as *Time* printed feature articles noting the growing emotional and physical toll of the war on the American and Iraqi populaces.[18] A growing antiwar protest outside of President Bush's ranch in Crawford, Texas, led by Cindy Sheehan, whose son was killed in combat in Iraq in April 2004, received a good deal of almost daily media attention during the late summer months of 2005.[19] Although not explicitly critical of the Bush administration, such stories do mark a shift in the larger American media's willingness to probe policy from different angles in a period when the government has been unusually vested in and controlling of what information about the war and U.S. military operations is available to the press.

This stands in marked contrast to the Vietnam War, of course, where the nightly news conveyed a constant raw and uncensored visual accounting of the human cost of the war and rising casualties, often providing a contradictory viewpoint to upbeat government propaganda about "winning the hearts and minds" of the Vietnamese people. Arguably, such extensive and immediate media coverage helped fuel antiwar opposition, including radical theatre protest, over a span of time during the first "living room" war. The current administration is much more media savvy and has artfully applied lessons of spin and control from the tensions of the earlier war reportage, vetted of course by conservative allies rooted in such network programs as Fox News. Nonetheless, as with past wars, the news media, as well as the larger entertainment industry, must eventually respond to such events, as evidenced in various emerging media contexts. For instance, the Web site ifilm.com recently introduced a new "channel" called WarZone, including unmediated video of military and political activities in Iraq.[20]

The generally slow-to-kindle debate over the validity of Bush's preemptive military strikes in Iraq, though, has perhaps softened the tone of some theatrical critiques of the war and presidential policy. In a March 5, 2004, profile in *Backstage* entitled "War Plays on NY Stages Still Proliferate with Insight, Passion," Leonard Jacobs canvassed various works that arguably could be perceived as war plays. Jacobs notes that "March 30 marks one year since U.S. and U.K. forces invaded Iraq [now over two years] and plays about war—its aftermath, its unceasing destruction—continue to be abundant on the NY Stage." Most of the early theatrical responses Jacobs refers to, however, approached the war from an allegorical perspective. He cites a number of productions revolving around a World War II context, such as David Auburn's Holocaust survivor drama *The Journals of Mihail Sebastian* at the Theater at 45th Street; Doug Wright's successful one-man play *I Am My Own Wife;* and Thirteenth Night Theatre Company's production of Robert David McDonald's *Summit Conference* (which explores the lives of Eva Braun and Clara Petacci, mistresses of Hitler and Mussolini). He also takes note of several plays dealing with the larger backdrop of Middle Eastern politics, such as William Gibson's *Golda* and Elaim Kraiem's *Sixteen Wounded,* both of which ran on Broadway. Revivals of classics that allow audiences to read aspects of the war in Iraq into the directorial and/or visual design concepts are perhaps most prolific on American stages. Jacobs cites downtown productions of Shakespeare's *Troilus and Cressida* with an antiwar message, the Aquila Theatre Company's *Othello* in a "contemporary military world," the Classical Theatre of Harlem's *Mother Courage,* and Theodore Skiptares's *Odyssey: The Homecoming* in March 2004 as representative and provocative examples of this kind of work.[21]

This trend continued well into the fall as a response to the hotly contested presidential campaign, as noted in a September 2004 *American Theatre* essay on the ways in which twenty companies nationwide chose to engage the political climate. Major regional theatres still seem focused on allegorical responses to international events like Portland Stage's *King Lear,* with director Chris Coleman noting that it is a "*Lear* prepared in the midst of suicide bombings, false intelligence on WMDs and the photos of Abu Ghraib."[22] One of the more interesting examples along these lines was the Alabama Shakespeare Festival's *Macbeth,* created to tour military bases as part of an NEA-funded program. Artistic director Kent Thompson's account of the obstacles faced in negotiating military bureaucracy suggests that a positive dialogue eventually emerged between the artists and their audiences, but in the planning stage he received "anxious" calls from military public relations officers wanting to ensure that "the show wasn't critical of our troops in Iraq."[23] However, a significant increase of new works created specifically to respond to, and in some cases criticize, American foreign policy and/or military involvement also seemed present in the theatre season around America. Prominent examples included John Green's *The Whole Thing* at Stage

Left Theatre in Chicago, which producing artistic director Kevin Heck-
man called a "rude, crude geopolitical farce that takes a hard look at
U.S. involvement in the Middle East and, more broadly, asks questions
about the path of this country since 9/11."[24]

Mark Crispin Miller's *Patriot Act: A Public Meditation*, which drew
on various documentary sources to present a "blistering attack" on the
current political establishment, echoes radical protest works such as *Viet
Rock*. While the polemical play was continually showcased at the New
York Theatre Workshop throughout fall 2004, interestingly enough artistic director Jim Nicola did not want the play to be seen as 1960s agitprop theatre: "we never expect audiences to embrace ideals wholesale—
we're not indoctrinating them. We say to them, 'You have to have an
opinion. You have to be informed. You have to think.'"[25]

Another smart, courageous play, the revival of John Weidman and
Steven Sondheim's surprisingly ironic musical *Assassins*, found a similarly receptive audience and also a glowing critical reception during its
run on Broadway at the Roundabout Theatre in the spring and summer
of 2004. Having probed the psyches of various presidential assassins
and would-be assassins as representatives of a disaffected and alienated
underclass of American society, *Assassins* was panned during its premiere
at Playwrights Horizons amid the patriotic support of America's initial
invasion of Iraq during the first Gulf War. In 1991 critics dismissed the
play as inappropriate given our military involvement overseas, a fact not
forgotten in 2001 when producers delayed the revival's opening for fear
the material was too inflammatory in the wake of 9/11. The show did
open two and a half years later on April 22, 2004,[26] but did not tour—a
clear indication of the substantial support felt for President George W.
Bush in the heartland. Yet the climate for the play's critical and audience
reception in New York was arguably perfectly timed. Although today's
Broadway audiences are more tourist-oriented than in past years, the
Roundabout run was buffered by a subscription audience that was no
doubt more politically willing to engage the play's politics than were
audiences in 1991 and by a larger atmosphere in New York during the
summer of 2004 that witnessed protests of varying kinds against the
arrival of the Republican Party for its National Convention in August
at Madison Square Garden.[27]

Had *Assassins* continued its run, as initially expected, into the late
summer months, it is doubtful that it would have found a place on the
list of "family values"–oriented Broadway musicals recommended to
party delegates. Indeed, Bush's spokesman Ken Lisaius refused to comment on the production, stating that "we don't offer theater reviews
from the White House. . . . We're focused on the war on terror and the

economy."[28] Despite the lack of critical endorsement from the White House, the play's relation to the zeitgeist was clear and aptly captured by former critic Frank Rich in his *New York Times* essay "At last, 9/11 Has Its Own Musical." Rich noted that a May 2004 opinion poll stated that 57 percent of Americans believed the United States to be "on the wrong track" and argued that in 1991 "the assassins on stage were also unthreatening—historical curiosities from distant dark ages of American turmoil."[29] The subject matter was clearly relevant enough to push emotional buttons in 1991, but Rich's point is well taken, given the palpable fear of violence by angry militants. Furthermore, as Weidman himself claimed in an interview, "the country is a far less comfortable and complacent place than it was. . . . In 1991 it seemed like a cheap trick when the actors pointed their guns at the audience. . . . [N]ow we all feel vulnerable" and like "potential targets."[30]

Despite the slow development of oppositional voices to the Iraq War in America, the 2004–5 theatre productions I have discussed were significant in their willingness to create a public forum for dialogue about controversial current events in a political climate where such discourse was sometimes very difficult. As Theatre Communications Group executive director Ben Cameron observed in his forum "Partisan Passions" last fall, civil and informed exchange about the war and election issues seemed almost impossible at times among commuters, family members, and friends. "[A]s a nation," Cameron wrote, "we are deeply, angrily divided, with a degree of passion I cannot remember in my lifetime." Of course, such a climate also clamors for a theatrical response to debate, to question and maybe even "accuse" at times in the tradition of the 1960s radical theatre. As Cameron said, "how we will display our comparable convictions . . . will be a question for the coming months. . . . Never has it been more important to take stands on the issues that divide us."[31] Along these lines, a number of New York–based artists did come together to create THAW, or Theatres Against the War. This organization mobilized theatres across the city to insert peace statements in programs and held a one-year anniversary benefit in 2004 where letters from soldiers stationed overseas were read by leaders in the arts community. A larger attempt at coordinating international theatre resources (often via the internet and email) was embodied by *The Lysistrata Project,* which generated more than one thousand readings and productions of Aristophanes' famous antiwar play worldwide.[32]

While such transgressive acts of political theatre are noteworthy and indicate a growing concern with foreign affairs in some artistic circles, the passion and even moral outrage that characterized much of the radical theatre of the 1960s seems lacking in such responses to the war in

Iraq. For instance, one of the darker political plays of recent times was the Riot Group's *Pugilist Specialist,* which premiered in the United Kingdom and was performed Off-Broadway in November 2004. In an interview with *nytheatre.com,* company member Adriano Shaplin was asked why the play, a work that revolves around four marines preparing for an assassination mission, does not mention the war in Iraq. He responded that the play was concerned with

> how a war begins as a story . . . or the ways in which language is a preface to violence. . . . As far as audiences go, I don't feel that I know more about the war than our average audience member. . . . I consider myself a political writer, but I will never write agitprop. I won't write propaganda. I won't congratulate the audience for having the correct opinion. In writing *Pugilist Specialist,* I tried to create a play that would be good ten years after the war.[33]

The Riot Group's deliberate avoidance of politics is well intentioned, as is James Nicola's desire not to preach to audiences at the New York Theatre Workshop. Radical artists from the 1960s such as Julian Beck and Judith Malina have long conceded that confrontational tactics and forced audience participation are now dated in an age characterized by postmodern irony and sound bite–driven media communication. Even so, I would contend that a vital theatrical response to current political events must not be afraid to establish a strong viewpoint that might include direct criticism or opposition to the Bush administration's policies and the war in Iraq. Also, given that the average contemporary viewer has been arguably desensitized to violence and that the bar on jarring audiences out of a deep-rooted political apathy (if not cultural nihilism) has grown increasingly higher since the 1970s, artists have to take risks and be willing to offend or anger audiences and critics in order to establish a legitimate critique of the war.

The radical theatre of the 1960s was the product of an authentic, urgent response to Vietnam and other troubling political events of that era. Companies such as the San Francisco Mime Troupe, Bread and Puppet Theater, and El Teatro Campesino all created highly topical street-theatre pieces. These radical works were often improvisatory and rooted in a raw, immediate reaction to current events, a quality that created a sense of vitality in the moment of the audience-performer encounter, one that was not concerned with literary rigor or canonical longevity.[34] For example, the Bread and Puppet Theater, founded by pacifist Peter Schumann in 1961, sought to raise the consciousness of its audiences regarding various inhumane events around the world. In the mid-1960s, however, Schumann focused his energies on protesting the war in Vietnam. Stefan Brecht contends that "what Schumann and the Peace Movement carried out into the streets of New York was the theme of war, and, to some—lesser—extent—its image." While groups like Davis's Mime Troupe performed "anti-war skits at rallies or by themselves in parks," Brecht credits Schumann with perfecting the practice of "parade art." Indeed, his giant puppets, which depicted various aspects of U.S. military involvement in Vietnam, were a common sight at many peace marches of this period. Beyond these street protests, however, Schumann also presented three specific plays in this period that denounced the war in Vietnam: *Fire* in 1966, *Wounds of Vietnam* in 1967, and *Bach Cantata #140* in 1967. Schumann also explored the ideology of violent resistance in his 1968 work *A Man Says Goodbye to His Mother*.[35] All of these plays reflected the radical politics of the day that often linked together the suffering of American minorities and Vietnamese civilians, thus offering up an ideologically complex critique of the Vietnam War in the context of corrupt domestic policies and imperialist foreign affairs. (Interestingly, such themes were also taken up in less avant-garde, but equally political and critical, plays of this period such as Vietnam veteran David Rabe's 1971 Broadway production *Sticks and Bones*.)[36] Again, most of these works were not created with the mind-set of longevity beyond their political relevancy in the here and now of the performance site, which might still be a relevant concern and reminder to current companies engaging the war in Iraq.

To date, the theatrical response to the war in Iraq has lacked the same urgency, but it remains to be seen if that will change among young theatre artists as the war continues and the casualty lists grow. A few veteran political theatre companies from the 1960s era, such as the Living Theatre and Bread and Puppet Theater, are still active today, although they, too, have responded to the war in a more cautious manner when compared to the heyday of 1960s radical theatre. The Living Theatre did respond with vigor to the Gulf War in its 1991 production of *The Rules of Civility*, which I worked on as an assistant director at the company's E. 3rd Street theatre. The play's thesis deployed a Brecht-style dialectic on the subject of George Washington's 110 "rules" of behavior.[37] Playwright-director Hanon Reznikov expressed a desire to expose "the rules" as a false veneer of civility that had been imposed over individual discourse and national and foreign policy in America, in place of a deeper, more truthful code of ethics, morality, or justice. Washington—and the country whose persona he represents in the play—claim to be altruistic but are in fact pursuing a self-interested perspective and set of policies. Thus, the play attempts to show a process whereby

America sculpted its image and national agenda in its infancy, a process that then extended internally through westward expansion and externally through empire building and economic imperialism.

During our rehearsals the Gulf War broke out, and consequently both Reznikov and the ensemble hoped to find some way to incorporate a pacifist-based criticism of America's military involvement into the production. The play's ending was thus rewritten for the ensemble to don camouflage cloth as they moved into the audience to confront the atavistic image of the elder (Tom Walker) and younger (Isha Beck) Washingtons onstage. Singing a refrain of "no more war" that built to a dramatic climax, the actors tore the "Desert Storm"–like material in collective protest as the "two Washingtons" cowered in fear onstage. Afterward, the audience was invited to partake in a silent, candlelight vigil held outside the theatre in protest of the war. Although this reflective postproduction event took place beyond the formal boundaries of the performance site, it succeeded in bringing the cast and lingering audience members together to consider the play's premise in relation to current world affairs.[38]

Although the Living Theatre has not yet produced a new work in response to American military involvement in Iraq, it did participate in various protest activities during the election season via a project called *Code Orange Cantata* (for example, a march from Union Square to Madison Square Garden entitled "Still We Rise March and Rally" on August 31, 2004, as well as a "Protest Rally During Bush Acceptance Speech" on September 2, 2004). The company is also currently in the midst of building a new theatre in Midtown Manhattan after a residency in Italy in recent years. Although plans have been delayed because of zoning issues, the troupe will be producing new politically oriented works in the near future. And while it, too, is interested in reaching a larger, more mainstream audience these days, as suggested by the chosen site of its new space, given the company's long-term commitment to promoting pacifism, its work will surely not hesitate to offer an oppositional voice to the war in Iraq. Similarly, Schumann's Bread and Puppet Theater continues to tour with new productions and in December 2004 presented a double bill of works that engaged various aspects of the current political climate at the Theater for the New City in New York. Bread and Puppet's *World on Fire* revolves around "a group of national emergency clowns" as they "demonstrate official reactions to the ultimate emergency (music by the Asymmetric Prisoner-of-War Orchestra)," whereas the less satirical *Daughter Courage* depicts the story of American activist Rachel Corrie, who died at the age of twenty-three in Palestine in 2003 as she tried to stop a bulldozer from destroying a Palestinian home.[39]

The continuing example and leadership of activists linked to the radical theatre of the 1960s is important to any notion of a contemporary political theatre, but it is important for younger artists to create works reflecting their own unique individual and collective voices to respond to the Iraq War and U.S. foreign policy. Furthermore, not all of the critical theatrical responses to the Vietnam War were scripted or presented in conventional, matrixed theatre spaces. Like Bread and Puppet's "parade art," some street encounters that expressed strong points of view were performative acts in their own right. To date, no major national protest against the current war in Iraq has emerged like the peace gathering in Washington, DC, during the Gulf War in 1991. However, the 1960s tradition of street political protest and performance was very present during the fall 2004 election, as there was a sizable demonstration outside the Republican National Convention on Sunday, August 29. The large-scale gathering included various kinds of marches and theatrical protests by groups such as the Imagine Festival of Arts, Ideas, and the UnConvention, which produced a provocative six-play politically oriented series. Republican delegates attended eight "family friendly" musicals and were greeted by protesters and hecklers outside the respective theatres. In addition, one organization, Shut It Down NYC, lobbied actors in these shows to boycott the performances and stated on their Web site that "the most significant impact we can have as New Yorkers during the convention is simply not showing up." Reflecting the change in our cultural landscape since the radicalism of the 1960s, Actors Equity president Alan Eisenberg advised cast members to go to work, stating, "Equity has a long-standing policy that the association does not endorse or take a position on any political candidate or party."[40]

Still, the larger global political climate encourages street performance and protest around the world, as evidenced by a striking photo spread in the *New York Times* entitled "Taking It to the Global Street."[41] Some fifteen hundred people also attended the Second International Congress on Victims of Terrorism in Bogotá, Colombia, during February 2005, representing "those who experienced terrorist attacks in Colombia, Indonesia, Israel, Spain, Northern Ireland, Chile, Argentina and Beslan, Russia." Domestically, the families of victims of the World Trade Center attacks have been visible in the political response to and investigation of those events. At the Colombia conference various organization leaders discussed "moving from the national scale to the international scale," and the World Trade Center United Family Group has recently begun correspondence with victims of the train attack in Madrid on March 11, 2005.[42] Such efforts to bridge cultural and national barriers in response to common concerns about international violence are vital and productive. Ben Cameron's comments about the need to create a similar consensus and dialogue are equally necessary here in America, although undeniably difficult in an ongoing postelection climate where extreme conservative forces seem empowered to encroach on freedom of expression. Interestingly, the NYC Police Department is now enforcing a "little-known regulation adopted four years ago that bans any parades on Fifth Avenue that were not permitted prior to July 2001." The implications of this ban are that a protest against the war in Iraq, of the sort that occurred during the Gulf War and Vietnam, would not be permissible in this historic parade route. Indeed, the "regulation surfaced in a lawsuit filed against the city by a group of anti-war demonstrators," as their proposal for an antiwar protest on March 19, 2005, was moved to a different route.[43] Although Mayor Bloomberg has defended the law based on protecting business concerns on Fifth Avenue, it does seem coincidental that the restrictions are only being enforced shortly after the well-publicized protests during the Republican Convention.

In early 2005 the Arts and Leisure section of the *New York Times* also ran a compelling feature entitled "Fighting Words," which conveyed how "defiant, resentful, scared soldiers in Iraq" were expressing their feelings and viewpoints through "rap" as a powerful new wartime performance medium or "weapon."[44] Mark Amitin, who worked with the Living Theatre during the late 1960s and 1970s, as well as creating the Universal Movement Theatre Repertory to help disseminate information about the radical theatre groups of the era, believes that the theatrical response to the war and current political situation is still in a relatively nascent stage. In his opinion, during the Vietnam era, major street protests and antiwar movements, as well as corresponding radical performances, took several years to develop major momentum. In that regard it has only been two years since the war's outbreak, and Amitin thinks that young people and various "downtown" theatre companies are gathering their energies in NYC and will begin responding more visibly, and critically, as our military presence in Iraq and elsewhere continues.[45]

Still, unlike the Vietnam era, more direct, potentially controversial representations of the war and its larger post-9/11 context seem to be centered on a flurry of projects developed for television and film. Both Warner Bros. and Beacon Communications are battling for the rights to bring the story of Daniel Pearl, who was kidnapped and murdered by militant extremists on videotape in Afghanistan in 2002, to the big screen. FX cable TV has just released a new series called "Over There," which tracks a unit of eight young soldiers fighting insurgents outside of Baghdad. Television veteran Stephen Bochco is the show's producer, and he gave a publicity statement, noting that FX created it because "Iraq is not a subject area that network television would be comfortable exploring because of the potential for conflict and controversy." Still, Bochco's cocreator and executive producer, Chris Gerolmo, expressed concern about the "politics" of the war, claiming to focus on the lives of the young soldiers in lieu of "policy makers or policy questions." Given how polarizing the general subject is in the United States right now, all concede that the show's content will inevitably "push buttons." The characters do respond to politically sensitive topics such as 9/11 and Abu Ghraib, but different viewpoints are represented, "much like the country." While this reticence to impose a position about the war echoes most of the theatre pieces discussed in my essay, the series and these films are engaging the war and issues of homeland security more directly and for a potentially larger target audience. (Not to mention the network TV series *24*, which was dominated last season by Islamic terrorists' attacks on American nuclear reactors.) In the wake of the London bombing attacks, Paramount is also developing a script called *Homeland*, which deals "with the impossible task of protecting a country with 12,383 miles of coastline from attacks."[46]

Not surprisingly, two high-profile plays in London right now are "tackling urgent contemporary issues, with both constructed by the same writer, Robin Soans, out of interviews with people directly affected by the subject matter." *The Arab-Israeli Cookbook* at the Tricycle Theatre describes a suicide bomber's attack on a bus in Jerusalem; whereas *Talking to Terrorists* at the Royal Court Theatre constructs an evening of theatre out of interviews with perpetrators of violence globally from Ireland to Uzbekistan to Iraq. Given our current climate that understandably tends to demonize terrorists, the latter play is arguably uncomfortable for audiences in its "topicality," by attempting to put a "human face" on these individuals and the causes, and effects, of terrorism.[47] In America the mainstream theatre community will likely continue to respond to the war and terrorist attacks in an allegorical fashion. As in the 1960s, however, smaller companies less dependent on box office increasingly seem to be cultivating a stronger, even oppositional voice to the war. For instance, the March 17, 2005, *Backstage* revealed casting ads for the following plays: Apanamae Production's multimedia play *I (Ran) to Iraq*, seeking seven "confident" actors—"one white male, two Arab males, one Arab female"—for a "poetic, political satire of the Iraq War."[48] Also, *Terrorism,* a more high-profile production at the John Houseman Theatre on 42nd Street by the Play Company, in conjunction with the New Group, was characterized as "six interconnected scenes" that "examine a society ravaged by terror" (with previous productions in London, Moscow, and throughout Europe).[49]

Clearly, as with the Vietnam War, we are still grappling individually and collectively with the impact and consequences of 9/11 and our subsequent military reactions overseas. As the war in Iraq and aesthetic responses in all media continue to unfold, we will clearly need to revisit these issues to absorb the clarity that time and historical distance allow. The healing years of the post-Vietnam era created a kind of political apathy that permeated both cultural life and artistic endeavors, but clearly the current state of world affairs, including the threat of another terrorist attack on the home front, has changed this dynamic for all Americans, including theatre artists. The radical theatre of the 1960s offers a vital inheritance to politically minded companies, yet art, theatre, and political protest must change and adapt to contemporary times and the specific context of our current military involvement in Iraq. Consequently, a variety of theatrical responses to current U.S. wars are expected and even healthy for the public discourse around such events. As they continue and most likely grow in volume and intensity as the cost of the war drags on, it is equally important for a free society to encourage, and support, oppositional and even overtly critical artistic works as well. Should our military involvement in Iraq linger long-term, hopefully those kinds of voices will also fully reemerge in the American theatre.

Notes

1. Lawrence H. Suid, *Guts & Glory: Great American War Movies* (Reading, MA: Addison-Wesley, 1978), 102–6.

2. J. W. Fenn, *Levitating the Pentagon: Evolutions in the American Theatre of the Viet Nam War Era* (Newark: University of Delaware Press, 1992), 50; Nora Alter, *Viet Nam Protest Theatre* (Bloomington: Indiana University Press, 1994), 6–7.

3. Richard Gilman, "Growing Out of the Sixties," *Performance* 1 (Dec. 1972): 25.

4. Todd Gitlin, *The Sixties: Years of Hope, Days of Rage* (New York: Bantam, 1987), 3.

5. Judith Malina, "Judith on the Revolution," *Yale/Theatre* 2 (spring 1969): 32.

6. Susan Jeffords, *Hard Bodies: Hollywood Masculinity in the Reagan Era* (New Brunswick, NJ: Rutgers University Press, 1994), 7.

7. "Were the Good Old Days That Good?" *New York Times,* July 3, 2005.

8. Richard Schechner, "The Decline and Fall of the American Avant-Garde," in *The End of Humanism,* ed. Barbara Schapiro (New York: Performing Arts Journal, 1982), 11–76.

9. Philip Auslander, *Presence and Resistance: Postmodernism and Cultural Politics in Contemporary American Performance* (Ann Arbor: University of Michigan Press, 1994), 26, 39, 37.

10. Richard Butsch, *The Making of American Audiences* (Cambridge, UK: Cambridge University Press, 2000), 293–94.

11. Jeffords, *Hard Bodies,* 12.

12. Raymond Hernandez and Patrick D. Healy, "The Evolution of Hillary Clinton," *New York Times,* July 13, 2005.

13. Frank Rich, review of *Archaeology of Sleep,* Living Theatre, New York, *New York Times,* January 19, 1984.

14. Sy Syna, review of *Rules of Civility,* by Hanon Reznikov, Living Theatre, New York, *Backstage,* March 22, 1991.

15. Howard Kissel, "Isn't the Living Theatre Dead Yet?" *Daily News,* May 18, 1989.

16. Mark Robinson, "Past Lives," review of *Mysteries and Smaller Pieces,* Living Theatre, New York, *Village Voice,* Sep. 20, 1994, no page number available.

17. Marvin Carlson, review of *Tight, Right, White,* by Reza Abdoh, as performed by Dar A. Luz, New York, *Journal of Dramatic Theory and Criticism* 8 (spring 1994): 187–91.

18. See, e.g., Damien Cave, "For Recruiters, a Hard Toll from a Hard Sell," *New York Times,* March 27, 2005; Eric Schmidt, "Army Likely to Fall Short in Recruiting, General Says," *New York Times,* July 24, 2005; and Nancy Gibbs, "The Lucky Ones," *Time,* March 21, 2005, 36–43.

19. Richard Stevenson, "Of the Many Deaths in Iraq, One Mother's Loss Becomes a Problem for the President," *New York Times,* Aug. 8, 2005.

20. Melvin Small, *Governing Dissent: The Media and the Anti-Vietnam War Movement* (New Brunswick, NJ: Rutgers University Press, 1994); Sarah Boxer, "See the War, after an Ad for the Army," Web site review, *New York Times,* Aug. 6, 2005.

21. Leonard Jacobs, "War Plays on NY Stages Still Proliferate with Insight, Passion," *Backstage,* March 5, 2004, 5.

22. Celia Wren, comp., "A Passion for Politics: Election Year on U.S. Stages," *American Theatre,* Sep. 2004, 20.

23. Kent Thompson, "Operation 'Macbeth,'" *American Theatre,* Feb. 2005, 27.

24. Quoted in Wren, "Passion for Politics," 23.

25. Megan Terry, *"Viet Rock" and Other Plays* (New York: Simon and Schuster, 1966), 88.

26. John Polly, *"Assassins* by Sondheim: 'Armed and Dangerous,'" *Next* 7 (April 2004): 13–15.

27. Jacobs, "War Plays on NY Stages," 40.

28. Barbara Hoffman, "Killer Comedy Shoots for a Funny Bone, Hits a Nerve," *New York Post,* April 8, 2004.

29. Frank Rich, "At Last, 9/11 Has Its Own Musical," *New York Times,* May 2, 2004.

30. Ibid.

31. Ben Cameron, "Partisan Passions," *American Theatre,* Sep. 2004, 4.

32. Leonard Jacobs, "Republican Confab Causes Theatrics," *Backstage,* Sep. 3–9, 2004, 1.

33. "NY Theatre Voices: Interview with Adriano Shaplin, *Pugilist Specialist,*" Oct. 25, 2004, www.nytheatre.com/nytheatre/voiceweb/v-shaplin.htm (accessed Dec. 9, 2005).

34. Theodore Shank, *American Alternative Theatre* (New York: St. Martin's, 1982), 60–71; R. G. Davis, *The San Francisco Mime Troupe: The First Ten Years* (Palo Alto, CA: Ramparts Press, 1975); Fenn, *Levitating the Pentagon,* 59–60; and El Teatro Campesino, *Vietnam Campesino, Theatre Three: The American Theatre, 1969–70* (New York: Scribner's, 1970), 150.

35. Stefan Brecht, *The Original Theatre of the City of New York from the Mid-Sixties to the Mid-Seventies: Book 4, The Bread and Puppet Theater,* vol. 1 (New York: Methuen, 1988), 476, 650–53, 664–71. See also Fenn, *Levitating the Pentagon,* 56; and Shank, *American Alternative Theatre,* 104–5.

36. David Rabe, *Sticks and Bones* (New York: Samuel French, 1972); *The Basic Training of Pavlo Hummel,* in *Famous Plays of the 1970s,* ed. Ted Hoffman (New York: Dell, 1981); Dick Brukenfeld, review of *Sticks and Bones,* by David Rabe, *Village Voice,* Nov. 11, 1971, clipping, Billy Rose Theatre Collection, Lincoln Center, New York.

37. Washington wrote these "rules" as a child, and they became the basis for a number of precepts that guided his career.

38. Hanon Reznikov, *The Rules of Civility and Decent Behavior in Company and Conversation,* as performed by the Living Theatre, New York, November 1990–February 1991; "The Rules of Civility," unpublished script with production staging notes, collection of the author.

39. December 2004 listings for *World on Fire* and *Daughter Courage,* produced by Bread and Puppet Theater, Theatre for the New City, New York, www.theatreforthenewcity.net.

40. Jacobs, "Republican Confab."

41. "Taking It to the Global Street," *New York Times,* March 20, 2005.

42. Glenn Collins, "Global Word to Terrorists: You Killed My Beloved," *New York Times,* March 20, 2005.

43. Mike McIntire, "A Ban on New 5th Avenue Parades? Who Knew?" *New York Times,* March 29, 2005.

44. Monica Davey, "Fighting Words," *New York Times,* February 20, 2005.

45. Mark Amitin, interview by the author, March 17, 2005, Montevallo, Alabama.

46. Christian Moerk, "The Race to Put Pearl on Screen," *New York Times,*

July 31, 2005; Allison Hope Weiner, "Licking and Salting War's Open Wounds," *New York Times,* July 25, 2005.

47. Mark Shenton, "London Calling: Terrorism On Stage and Off," *Backstage,* March 17, 2005, 34.

48. Casting Call, *Backstage,* March 17, 2005, 9.

49. Ibid., 22.

Identity as Ideology, Assumed or Otherwise

Second-Wave Responses to the Idea of 9/11

Evan M. Bridenstine

> Collective identities, whether they are cultural/ethnic, national, or even transitional, grow from a sense of the past; the theatre very forcefully participates in the ongoing representations and debates about these pasts, sometimes contesting the hegemonic understanding of the historical heritage on the basis of which these identities have been constructed, sometimes reinforcing them.
>
> —Freddie Rokem, *Performing History*

I N *Performing History* Freddie Rokem makes no case for privileging the "actual" or "authentic" in theatre that takes history as its subject; instead, he identifies history onstage as a re-creation or redoing, a questioning or confirming of how the past is to be interpreted.[1] At no point does theatre intend to become the history it represents, but performance sets theatrical energies in play when an audience shares a past that its collective identity has interpreted or is in the process of interpreting. Rokem does not view the outcome of this process as predetermined, but he does assume the presence of a collective identity or community engaged in "representations and debates about these pasts." However, in the case of theatre based on the September 11 terrorist attacks in New York City and Washington, DC, the interpretation of those events has begun with examinations of national, religious, and political identities as they relate to personal identification, concomitantly locating the community and calling for communal interpretations, while locating the individual as both in and out of alignment with communal ideologies.

Within the first year following September 11, 2001, a large number of theatrical responses emphasized individual testimony that offered an accounting of the artist's relationship to that event, contrasting "before" and "after." Many of these works also commemorated those who had died in the attacks, frequently noting the absence of persons whose presence had gone unnoted "before." Anne Nelson's *The Guys* provides an example of the prevalent trope of presence pointing to absence, of moving the artist into the subject position (in art) in order to somehow "speak" for those displaced (in life). Nelson's own experiences in helping a fire captain write eulogies for members of his company formed the basis of her "authority" as a speaker for all firemen in New York City; her choice to obscure or hide the identities of the "actual" firemen in order to preserve their families' privacy notwithstanding, the central narrative is that of Joan, Nelson's scripted self.[2] This approach to the topic of 9/11 allowed theatre artists to enter into a stream of discourse with other, nontheatrical, commemorations such as the publication of 9/11 memorials in the *New York Times* and formalized removals of remains from the Site. Identification and commemoration became an initial trope of September 11: commemoration of the dead, identification of the self within the context of "before" and "after" a specific loss. Identification with "we" often carried with it the associations found in trauma recovery—associating with those who share similar, if not exactly the same, injuries or standing in kinship with the dead.[3] Such identification created its own truncated language; "the Site," and "9/11" were spoken as understood or common-knowledge terms as that sense of kinship spread through post-9/11 discourse. It is typical for characters in 9/11-themed scripts to use a similarly truncated language, referring to the attacks as "the thing," "this," or even "it," often as a means of evasion. The assumption in both cases (life and art) is that the audience understands the referent, that if "you" are part of "us," you understand "it."

Almost immediately, the act of identification became politicized. Less than a week after the attacks, President Bush made the now famous declaration, "I can hear you. The rest of the world hears you, and the people who knocked these buildings down will hear all of us soon."[4] Bush's progression from "I" to "you" to "us" created a simple, apparent bond of identification: "I" identify "you" and align the two into an "us" that stands in opposition to "them."[5] To some extent Bush's declaration extended the politicized identification strategy that had begun in Broadway theatres with choruses of "God Bless America" earlier in the week, and both acts had provided an easy, if momentary, alignment through applause or song.

However inevitable or apparent that identification might have been,

at least two oral history accounts of Bush's visit relate weaknesses within
his rhetorical strategy. Through the story of Brian Lyons, Steven Brill
records a conflict of "identities" in play on the day Bush spoke to the
recovery workers: "The firemen were still looking for their missing
brothers, while the construction crews were trying to clear away the
wreckage."[6] As a construction worker whose brother was still missing,
Lyons identified with both groups and served as a kind of diplomat
between the two, but neither "us" did or could include Bush; as for
politics Lyons's immediate concern aligned him with the firemen searching for survivors, not the construction workers' attempts to make the
Site safe, but, although both groups cheered Bush's declaration, neither
prioritized action against "them" over the completion of their recovery
work. In his first-person account of the day, Dennis Smith acknowledges:

> I am reassured that the president is not voicing an idle threat. I know that
> he will take action, and I know we all have to remain patient, as he advises.
> Yet there is a new, ambiguous feeling I get when I think about the military
> consequence of Ground Zero, something I have never felt before. Like
> many of my friends, I am simply waiting for the other shoe to drop. What
> will be next? Will it be our move or theirs? This is not an ordinary war.[7]

For Smith a hierarchy exists within the "us" that Bush evoked; "he"
(in this case Bush) leads "us," takes action, and voices threats, while
"we" remain patient and, therefore, passive. Smith's "ambiguous feeling" connects to this hierarchy, this acknowledgment that although wars
are not led by "us," "we" or "they" will inevitably move against each
other even if a current referent for "them" remains unspecified. This
ambiguity in the midst of politicized identification, and the concomitant instability of such identification, opens a thread of discourse related
not to "facts" but to the interpretation of facts, not of what history is
but of what history means.

Although the early works of testimony privileged the commemoration trope, some also acknowledged issues related to politicized identification. In Nelson's *The Guys* the character of Joan finds the meaning
of 9/11 defined in terms of nation; the Argentineans she encounters
assert that the "American imperialists" who died in the attacks deserved
their fate, a position they adopt within a nationalized context. Joan tells
the audience:

> I couldn't wait to get back to New York. Where everyone understood. But
> I kept thinking about it. I realized that everything the Argentines were

saying was about their own war twenty years ago. They thought it was about them. Everybody, all over the world, was talking about it. Writing about it. And they all—they all—thought it was about them! But it's not. It's about us! Isn't it?[8]

Having faced an "us" that does not include her, Joan assumes that "they" have misinterpreted the meaning of the historical event, that only those involved (New Yorkers) could understand. Joan's "Isn't it?" assumes a stable national interpretation of what appear to be "obvious facts," but Nelson does not answer Joan's question. Instead, both Nelson and Joan complete their commemoration of the fallen, leaving Joan (and, possibly, the audience) unsettled at plot's end.

> TWO YEARS LATER: Though some were written soon after the planes hit the World Trade Center, plays which took the events of Sept. 11 as their inspiration didn't ascend New York stages in numbers until this year, which began with Neil LaBute's *The Mercy Seat* and ended with the triple bill of Craig Wright's *Recent Tragic Events,* Jonathan Bell's *Portraits,* and Theresa Rebeck and Alexandra Gersten-Vassilaros' *Omnium Gatherum.* All dealt with the tragedy in a somewhat oblique fashion and most critics agreed that a significant 9/11 drama has yet to surface.[9]

Within this summary of major theatre stories for 2003, Robert Simonson adopts a fairly common strategy by identifying the four plays as starting and ending points, thereby classifying them as a unified group on the basis of content ("plays which took the events of Sept. 11 as their inspiration"), treatment of that content ("a somewhat oblique fashion"), and chronological placement ("this year"). There are grounds for rejecting such a classification, if only because it assumes change based on production dates and not periods of script development outside of New York. However, such a statement also assumes that strategies employed during the first year's works of testimony have been abandoned in the second year's productions. Neither of those assumptions is accurate: additional *Playbill On-Line* articles publicize productions before and after the presumed starting and ending productions, including several works of testimony during that period.[10] Therefore, instead of assuming a clean break between the first and second years of production, it would be more accurate to state that a second wave had overlapped the first or that a second strategy had found production alongside the first. Even so, the four scripts that Simonson singles out have occupied a privileged position in discussions of 9/11 works, and each has been published in either reading or acting editions, which grants them accessibility unavailable to works as yet unpublished or unproduced outside of New York. Therefore, while acknowledging the presence of a great many scripts and productions not named here, this study will examine those four works as examples of the second wave or strategy.

These scripts do not use the "presence/absence" trope as Nelson and other early theatrical responders had done. Only one of the four presents any claim to the "authentic" or the "actual" professed by the earlier works of testimony; however, any deaths related to 9/11 in these scripts are fictive, even generic or aggregate. Instead of responding to the experience of 9/11, these scripts respond to the idea of 9/11. As for issues of identification, the attempt to locate "I" inside "we" foregrounds the instability of any "we" that might be evoked. Both "we" and "they" serve less as a means of trauma recovery (defining the self within a group) and more as a means of national or cultural alignment (defining the self against a group). Identity equates with ideology, revealing the self as always already politicized; to be so aligned equates the self with a set of ideas and not geography, with an assumed set of cultural attitudes and not demonstrated beliefs (questioned or unquestioned). In defining or redefining themselves, characters in these scripts negotiate the gaps where such ideological assumptions do not fully "fit." As a result of this negotiation, many of the major characters seem undefined, unresolved, or undone by the process, and the scripts themselves seem either unfinished or unsatisfying.

Along with the assumed presence of a "collective identity" engaged in the interpretation or reinterpretation of a shared past, Rokem acknowledges a dynamic process inherent within performance, particularly in performances based on historical events. The actor does not become the figure from the past; instead "the actors serve as a connecting link between the historical past and the 'fictional' performed here and now of the theatrical event," a function that recreates the actor as a "hyper-historian," a kind of witness to or of history through whom both past and present exist.[11] Performance of history thus opens discourse through "a constant mingling of ontological spheres, which as a rule do not coexist to the same extent in other contexts . . . to make them interact and in certain cases even, at least for a moment, to unify them completely" (191). Such a complete unification cannot be sustained, and the resulting destabilization provides a means of viewing or reviewing interpretations of history. Through this reasoning Nelson has set theatrical energies in motion in *The Guys* because she not only recorded her experience but also fictionalized it, and Sigourney Weaver's portrayal of Joan recreates Weaver as the hyper-historian of Nelson's experience; Nelson and Weaver enact a history that both is and is not the past, thereby opening discourse about that past. When the theatre artist does not occupy the subject position, when the authenticity of the artist's "actual" experience does not inform or guide the discourse, the theatre must then employ a different set of conflicting ontological spheres in order to question or reaffirm the meaning of 9/11. In the case of the "second wave" of 9/11 scripts the performance of history questions the stability of national identity by presenting as concomitant conflicting referents of both "us" and "them" even when (perhaps especially when) foregrounding the fictive over the factual.

In *The Mercy Seat* the character Ben Harcourt considers the possibility of letting his wife and children believe that he has died in the attacks; he considers this while hiding out in a condo owned by Abby Prescott, his lover and superior at work. In order to make a clean break, he cannot leave or be seen, nor can he answer his cell phone or place a call himself. His choice involves removing himself from one identity (father and husband) to create another. While in the process of making this decision, poised between identities, he is unable to align himself with Abby or even with other New Yorkers or Americans. His assertion that "I feel like everybody else does"[12] does not hold when Abby questions his unwillingness to act on those feelings through helping others, something "everybody else" seems to be doing; to be fair, Abby follows a woman who posts photocopies of a man's picture but does not offer to help her, so one can—as Ben does—question her identification as part of "everybody else." Ben defends his inaction by invoking his nationalized identity: "do you honestly think we're not gonna rebound from this? And I don't just mean you and me, I'm saying the country as a whole. Of course we will." However optimistic his assertion might seem, he offers it in a context of life returning to "the World Series, and Christmas, and all the other crap that you can count on in life," and he defines "the American way" as "to overcome, to conquer, to come out on top. And we do it by spending and eating and screwing our women harder than anyone else" (16). Abby rejects this definition, placing at least a portion of Ben's planned reidentification in peril by comparing Ben to two groups: those who are trying to help others or at least would like to be doing so and those who have become heroes by perishing in the attacks. Ultimately, Ben does not belong to either group, and his plan to take advantage of the situation by ending one life and beginning another divides him from Abby as well. The argument between them—over the attacks, over his plan, over her conduct at work, over his preferred sexual acts—leads to the end of their relationship. There is no "us," and this lack of alignment leaves Ben isolated at the end of the play, broken off from Abby yet unable to answer his cell phone and reassert his prior identity. He remains, as he protests as Abby leaves the condo, "just a little lost right now" (69).

In his preface to the Faber and Faber reading edition Neil LaBute states, "I hold the mirror up higher and try to examine how selfishness can still exist during a moment of national selflessness" (x). Although LaBute questions these conflicting impulses, he does not question their coexistence; however, if "national selflessness" does not preclude selfishness, can selflessness be a national characteristic? While such a brutal questioning of human behavior (even a brutal interpretation of human behavior) is not unique within LaBute's work, the brutality of *The Mercy Seat* maintains selflessness as absent: only the dead are heroes, and the living selfless are active outside Abby's condo, where the audience cannot see them. Using an identification strategy similar to President Bush's declaration from Ground Zero, LaBute's introductory comments invert Ben's optimism:

> I am trying to examine the "ground zero" of our lives, that gaping hole in ourselves that we try to cover up with clothes from The Gap, with cologne from Ralph Lauren, with handbags from Kate Spade. Why are we willing to run a hundred miles around simply saying to someone, "I don't know if I love you anymore"? Why? Because Nikes are cheap, running is easy, and honesty is the hardest, coldest currency on the planet. (x)

To paraphrase both LaBute and Ben, "we" consume more than we give, and selflessness is the exception. The potential discourse opened within this work locates the instability of "we" within this conception of "American" as a national signifier; as accounts of heroic rescues and insurance fraud have shown, both selflessness and selfishness are "us."

At the beginning of the acting edition of *Recent Tragic Events*, Craig Wright includes the following quote from Schopenhauer's *On the Apparent Design of Fate in the Individual*:

> All the events in a person's life would accordingly stand in two fundamentally different kinds of connection: firstly, in the objective, causal connection of the natural process; secondly, in a subjective connection which exists only in relation to the individual who experiences it, and which is thus as subjective as his or her own dreams. . . . That both kinds of connection exist simultaneously, and the selfsame event, although a link in two totally different chains, nevertheless falls into place in both, so that the fate of one individual invariably fits the fate of the other, and each is the hero of their own drama while simultaneously figuring in a drama foreign to

him—this is something that surpasses our powers of comprehension, and can only be conceived as possible by virtue of the most wonderful pre-established harmony.[13]

This duality allows for a double view of any event, even if the double view produces a double meaning. If events are both causal and relative, the debate over meaning will also be causal and relative or, in terms of the current discussion, both personal and national. When an event in one life intersects with another, the meaning of that event depends on the position of the subject. The inclusion of this quotation is itself an illustration of this concept: unless this quote is made available to the audience, only the production team can adopt the concept as a point of view informing the performance of the script. Even if the quotation is available, only those audience and production team members who actually read it can adopt this point of view and derive any "meaning" for the experience from that position.

Recent Tragic Events creates a dual experience dependent on the relative positions of audience and performer. At the start of the first act, the Stage Manager asks an audience member to toss a coin, thereby setting into play a series of choices determined by the random result. The Stage Manager informs the audience that moments determined by the coin toss will be identified by a tone: "The actors will not stop performing when the tone is sounded; the characters in the play will continue in blissful ignorance without pause. But you in the audience will know that those particular moments could potentially have occurred differently, or been omitted altogether, with other moments in their place" (9). The audience is thus positioned to read the performance as random, regardless of the significance of that influence; for example, one such moment involves pizza toppings. However, the script contains no alternative events, no deletions or substitutions; instead, the tone identifies points of decision. Therefore, the "chance" interpretation afforded to the audience is not an option for the performers. Wright reverses these positions for the second act. The Stage Manager addresses the audience again, but this time to announce that the tone changed none of the events of the first act. Instead, the Stage Manager states, "No matter how free the characters might seem, they never are. They're trapped. And nothing they do can stop *Recent Tragic Events* from proceeding toward its predetermined conclusion; predetermined, of course, because it is already *written*" (37). Having prepared the audience for an absence of chance, Wright then provides several moments in which the actors are instructed to improvise: one character has the instruction "describes book" (39), and a group is to create an "Oompa-Loompa kind of tune" (42). Although these improvisations do not come at moments of choice, the possibility of "chance" moves from audience to performance.

The action of *Recent Tragic Events* foregrounds the possibility of viewing 9/11 as simultaneously random and predetermined. Andrew arrives at Waverly's apartment to keep a blind date on September 12 and finds her trying to contact her twin sister, Wendy, who lives in New York City. As the evening passes, he faces a series of apparent connections between their lives and concludes that his choices have led him inevitably to her:

> "I mean, of course I went to school with Gerald Ittner, right? . . . And of course Waverly knows him too, and of course we have *both* managed to stay friends with him even though he has this English accent thing which *no one else* can bear— . . . And of course I went to New York and met Wendy because of course *another* friend had to change his life and teach music after being a stockbroker, *he* had no choice, he was doomed by his own integrity to do that, and now of course I show up tonight, and of course she reads Trollope and is the most perfect girl I've ever met. . . . Because Wendy was just as beautiful, of course, but way too . . . wild for me, I mean I hardly knew her, but I could tell by some of the things she said that she was out there. . . . *I'm saying I don't know where the chances stop and the choices start anymore!*" (47)

As a result of this "of course" litany, Andrew questions the existence of free will. He asks the then present Joyce Carol Oates, "if all those moments are connected, then aren't all moments connected, don't they have to be? And if they are, then where's the free will, where's the room for it?" Joyce then counters, "You're the one who's creating the perception of inevitability because it suits your purposes for some reason, not the other way around" (48). Waverly's neighbor Ron enters the argument by claiming that the United States' conduct does not allow for surprise, that acts taken by the nation had made the attacks inevitable; therefore, responses to the contrary force the speaker to agree to a preexisting scripting already existing in the mind. Neither Joyce nor Ron is willing to change their point of view, and Wright grants reasonable logic to both sides, thereby providing a dramaturgical illustration of the Schopenhauer quote. Joyce seems to gain an advantage by asking Ron, "So you're a puppet?" (51); however, the character of Joyce Carol Oates is a sock puppet manipulated by an otherwise mute character. Thus, the visual elements contradict the verbalized logic: Joyce is a manipulated object and therefore not possessed of free will. Ron's passionate argument for fate dissipates as soon as the debate ends. Before he leaves, Ron encourages Andrew and Waverly to keep "being Americans. Whatever that means" (54). The unsettled argument and the unspecified meaning of nation leave the discourse open. Are we to accept an argument for free will from a hand puppet? Are we to accept an argument for the inevitable consequences of national responsibility from a character who does not have a solid definition of *nation*? Can we reconcile these views even if the characters cannot?

A similar yet simpler contradiction informs Jonathan Bell's *Portraits*. To present a series of four monologues and one duologue, Bell creates frames that exist on two levels: his central character—an artist named Andrew—who imagines the lives of those "outside" of the attacks and a setting that features a large frame through which those imagined characters emerge to tell their stories. Having witnessed the fall of the Towers from his studio, Andrew finds himself unable to assist rescue efforts or to even go near the Site; for this reason, he says, "I continue to feel like an outsider. . . . [T]he only ones I could relate to were people on the outside, the perimeter. . . . I never saw their faces, but my dreams brought their lives into focus."[14] Each of the "portraits" Andrew then "draws" tells a story that by now might seem generic (at worst) or universal (at best): a woman in Oneida feels the need to talk to someone in New York and decides to call her own number, substituting "212" for the area code; a man's affair keeps him out of the office, which spares his life, but his wife's call to his cell phone betrays the affair, thus separating him from her Irish family of cops and firemen; an EMT from Boston heads into New York to help and finds that the work unites not only those from other cities but also those from other countries; a woman seeks out the wife of the man who died saving her son.

Only the fourth monologue, that of a Muslim woman named Arifa, makes any claim to authenticity through "actual" experience: introductory pages state that this monologue is based on Reshma Yaqub's article "You People Did This" (3). Each "portrait" speaks of forming a connection that identifies them with others, but Arifa's monologue deals most directly with the politicized identification of national signifiers. She identifies herself as both American and Muslim and tells of being attacked from both groups: "First, as Americans, by those madmen who struck our nation. Secondly, we were accused by some Americans who believe that all Muslims are accountable for those horrific acts" (24). Her response to the attacks was, therefore, personal: in fear of retaliation she moves to protect her sons. She speaks of violence against Muslims that came as a response to the attacks and to the Oklahoma City bombing, thus railing against one identification; she then protests that her religion and its language have been co-opted, that "jihad" signifies a "struggle to please God" (25–26), not holy warfare, thus railing against her other identification. To reconcile her crisis, she pronounces a sort of resolution: "Yes, there were martyrs made that day, but there were no terrorists among them. There were only Americans of every race and religion, who on that day gave their lives for all of us" (26). To some extent she removes one identity by repudiating claims regarding Islam, distancing herself from the terrorists by denying them inclusion in "Muslim"; through this denial she privileges "American" as her national signifier, thereby offering herself for inclusion within "us." However, this claim begins to falter even as it is spoken: has Arifa revised or interpreted 9/11 through this rhetorical negotiation? If lives are taken, have they been given?

A similar instability occurs at the conclusion of *Portraits*. Having provided introductions to each of the sections, Andrew interprets their meaning for his audience: "How could I ever think of myself as an outsider? None of us are any more. . . . The wind . . . is the souls of all of them, the spirit of all of us, the survivors . . . You and I" (40–41). The portrait characters reappear within the picture frame, and Andrew joins them, claiming that their creation has been "a tribute to the brave and lost, and those of us who survived" (41). Through these pronouncements Andrew offers an identification strategy to the audience: the "outside" is actually the "inside"—in fact, neither "outside" nor "inside" exists. However, since he has entered the frame shared by his portraits, that architectural piece now stands between him and the audience, creating a literal "inside" and "outside." His benediction sounds as murky as Arifa's earlier statement: "Let us not fall into the caverns of fear, brutality and darkness. . . . Breathe deeply. . . . Let the light into your life" (41). Since this character remains unable to connect with a world outside of his imagination, what is an audience to infer other than a hazy encouragement to avoid negative emotions?

In the early moments of *Omnium Gatherum* dinner party guests respond to two events: a "pre-appetizer" served by Suzie, their hostess, and a list in which the world's population is statistically reduced to a population of one hundred. Responses to the food interrupt the recitation of the list, establishing a commingling of excessive food and politically charged conversation during which the guests eat elaborate dishes and talk without listening. National and political identifiers settle on the dinner guests with a distinct lack of subtlety, and it would be easy and even on point to examine nothing more than the rigor with which the characters defend, define, and debate the meaning of these signifiers. Roger is the prototypical American capitalist warmonger and popular novelist who asserts that "we have to get a little crazy on everybody" in order to remain the leading world power.[15] Suzie is the domestic entrepreneur who believes eating is a spiritual activity; more than one reviewer identified Suzie as a Martha Stewart clone, which dovetails nicely with Suzie's love of and faith in television. Julia is the African American minister who writes on creativity and community yet finds herself "the only black person in the room" (31). Terrence is the British intellectual whose superior education provides him with witticisms and evasions but no basis for religious faith. Lydia is the feminist and vegan who believes war is a product of male narcissism. Jeff is the fireman, a simple man lost in complex conversation. The scholar Khalid and the terrorist Mohammed represent the Arab nations from seemingly polarized positions.

Perhaps more so than in the other scripts under consideration here, *Omnium Gatherum* highlights the assumptions attached to these signifiers, reversing some while apparently letting others remain. Roger's assumptions regarding Lydia's feminism offer one example of reversing assumptions. Roger concludes his response to her critique of Muslim culture with the accusation, "You want the whole world to look just the way you like it for you and your little proto-feminist lesbian friends" (50–51). However, Roger's conflation of feminism and lesbianism—a position shared by most of the other guests—does not hold when Lydia reveals that she is in a long-term relationship with one man and pregnant with another man's child. After confessing this, she claims, "I want the world to be whole. I want women to be included. That doesn't mean I hate men. 'Hating men' is hardly my problem" (58). However, Roger's assumptions regarding Arabs prevent him from distinguishing between Khalid and Mohammed: after Mohammed is physically subdued, Roger mutters, "Those crazy Muslims" (62), a signifier that includes Khalid, who has criticized capitalism throughout the evening. Although they may question their assumptions, characters do not seem to change their beliefs; instead, they may (as Roger does) simply dismiss the argument with a grunt or choose (as Lydia does) isolation over agreement, dismissing Roger with the statement, "I am so not in community with you" (35). All the dinner guests find themselves ideologically isolated, unable to agree on any subject other than the taste of the "pre-appetizer" that began the meal.

The consequences of this isolation are most apparent in moments of physical threat. At various points in the evening, helicopters and explosions interrupt the conversation, but no one takes action; final stage directions indicate, "In the distance, the rumble of faint explosions can be heard. The explosions get closer and closer until one loud, terrifying

explosion bathes the room in a sudden white light" (74). In addition
to this threat the guests slowly realize that they might be dead and in
hell. Although the guests wonder whether they should or even can do
anything, they choose to ignore the danger as stridently as they ignore
each other. As the explosions approach, they dance, smoke, kiss, and
eat. "They" should do something, shouldn't "they"? Wouldn't "we"?

A man sits in his mistress's condo, unable to leave one life, one identity, to create another. A man and woman on a blind date find themselves unable to determine where choices end and fate begins. An artist
imagines the experiences of a world he has been unable to rejoin. A
group of party guests choose to isolate themselves rather than adapt
their thinking. Each of these responses to 9/11 opens discourse about
the meaning of that event, and each leaves that discourse suspended.
If, as Rokem suggests, theatrical representations of history provoke discourse, then the results of that discourse are not predetermined, but
the provocation within these scripts centers around unsympathetic characters, inconsistent logic, and complicated production elements. Perhaps
we haven't finished processing the history shaping our collective identity. Perhaps making the case for the instability of national signifiers
prevents or precludes deeper conclusions than "We should do something" or "We should try to get along." Perhaps no collective identity
is present to process or interpret. That questions should be asked, that
assumptions should be questioned, that action should be taken, and that
discourse should avoid the easy solutions would seem to be the achievement and impact of the "second wave."

Notes

1. See Freddie Rokem, *Performing History: Theatrical Representations of
the Past in Contemporary Theatre* (Iowa City: University of Iowa Press, 2000),
esp. 3.

2. Evan M. Bridenstine, "The View from Where? Identity, Borrowed
Speech, and Obscured Presence in Anne Nelson's *The Guys,*" *Text and Presentation* 24 (April 2003): 127–37.

3. Judith Herman, *Trauma and Recovery: The Aftermath of Violence—
From Domestic Abuse to Political Terror* (New York: Basic Books, 1997). In the
reading edition of *The Guys* Anne Nelson points to this reprint of Herman's
1972 text. Of particular interest, regarding the current discussion, is chapter 10,
"Reconnection."

4. Quoted in Steven Brill, *After: How America Confronted the September
12 Era* (New York: Simon and Schuster, 2003), 64.

5. On this point I am indebted to Bruce McConachie's reading of Kenneth

Burke, "Using the Concept of Hegemony to Write Theatre History," in *Interpreting the Theatrical Past,* ed. Thomas Postlewait and Bruce McConachie (Iowa City: University of Iowa Press, 1989), 37–58. Burke's concept of the "assumed we" is particularly relevant here.

6. Brill, *After,* 64.

7. Dennis Smith, *Report from Ground Zero* (New York: Viking, 2002), 206.

8. Anne Nelson, *The Guys* (New York: Random House, 2002), 47–48.

9. Robert Simonson, "Playbill On-Line Selects the Top Theatre Stories of 2003," *Playbill On-Line,* December 29, 2003, http://www.playbill.com/features/article/83529.html (accessed Nov. 1, 2005).

10. The Present Company's production of *Stories about What Happened* opened in May 2002, and Arthur Laurents's *Attacks on the Heart* at the George Street Playhouse closed in November 2003. "This year" seems fairly long.

11. Rokem, *Performing History,* 13. Subsequent page references to this source will be provided parenthetically in the text.

12. Neil LaBute, *The Mercy Seat* (New York: Faber and Faber, 2003), 11. Subsequent page references to this source will be provided parenthetically in the text.

13. Craig Wright, *Recent Tragic Events* (New York: Dramatists Play Service, 2004), 7. Subsequent page references to this source will be provided parenthetically in the text.

14. Jonathan Bell, *Portraits* (New York: Samuel French, 2004), 8–9. Subsequent page references to this source will be provided parenthetically in the text.

15. Theresa Rebeck and Alexandra Gersten-Vassilaros, *Omnium Gatherum* (New York: Samuel French, 2003), 21. Subsequent page references to this source will be provided parenthetically in the text.

Stephen Sondheim's *Assassins* and the Wartime Political Climate

Diana Calderazzo

I N STEPHEN SONDHEIM'S darkly comic musical vaudeville *Assassins* (1991), the main characters sing "everybody's got the right to their dreams." Although this phrase may seem a basic reflection of the American way, alongside ballpark anthems and apple pie, it adopts chilling irony when placed in the mouths of those who have attempted to kill a U.S. president. This irony is exactly what Sondheim and librettist John Weidman achieve in *Assassins,* which presents a chronicle of American presidential assassination from the point of view of the assassins themselves. From this jarring perspective the show points to the bleaker aspects of American society, assessing the social milieu that breeds thoughts of assassination. Although critical perception in the United States during the Gulf War first labeled the show as a distasteful and mostly pointless chronicle of an American aberration, more recent reviews and discussions both at home and abroad have recognized the piece as an important commentary on global social awareness. Produced around the world, *Assassins* has challenged critics and audiences to re-evaluate their notions of patriotism, their sensitivity to self-deprecating satire, and their impressions of domestic versus global political events. In addressing themes of such a controversial nature, the show has demonstrated the ways in which audience perception can shape itself in response to the prevailing political atmosphere.

By the time composer-lyricist Sondheim wrote *Assassins,* his firmly established reputation defined him as one of the most ingenious writers of dark musical comedy in the modern era, his innovations surpassing even the eerie counter rhythms of Kurt Weil and the bold, mimicking tones of Kander and Ebb. His 1970 musical *Company* is said to have refined and epitomized the concept musical, centering on the exploration of a central idea, that of marriage, rather than on a driving story or plotline. Employing sardonic lyrics and musical pastiche, Sondheim juxtaposed traditional romantic images of marriage with less romantic undertones that were largely considered taboo in musical comedy. In the same vein jarringly unconventional topics became the focus of Sondheim's subsequent works, many of which asked audiences to view themselves as contributing factors within their social environments.[1]

When *Assassins* debuted at Playwrights' Horizons on January 27, 1991, critics and audiences were at least partially accustomed to Sondheim's grotesque humor and the intellectual challenges his pieces offered in musical form. In this new musical Sondheim asked audiences to question the traditional definition of the American Dream, to objectively consider not only the success stories but also the misfits underneath the surface of American prosperity, and to question their own roles in a society that produces such misfits. The "misfits" are the nine lead characters, based on the nine historical figures that have attempted (successfully in four cases) to assassinate American presidents; and they are as close to being protagonists as the indifferent Bobby in *Company* or the bloodthirsty Sweeney in *Sweeney Todd*. The main difference, according to critic Geoffrey Block writing for *American Music* in 1993, is that these previous characters are fictitious, whereas the assassins are an all-too-real element of American history.[2] The factual foundations of these characters and their actions allow a direct and unmitigated presentation of a horrible truth that many American viewers would rather forget. Moreover, *Assassins* asks viewers to evaluate their own roles in a society that has allowed this truth to exist, a considerable challenge for audiences of any nationality, much less those who identify as citizens of a country as traditionally patriotic as the United States of America.

Not only did *Assassins* address serious and controversial social concerns within a historically accurate context; it did so through the utilization of a lighthearted pastiche of romantic American musical references not unlike the romantic recollections of couples' dances in *Company*. Indeed, the structure of the piece as a whole reflects that of the American vaudevilles of the 1930s, in which each performer would present a skit, song, or monologue in turn, ending with a group song-and-dance presentation, a widely acceptable format if the characters are not psychopathic killers. In *Assassins,* however, Giuseppe Zangara complains of stomach sickness brought on by the unfair distribution of opulence in society, resulting in his avowal to kill President Roosevelt. Meanwhile, Samuel Byck laments the lack of sensitivity in society and reveals his plan to kill President Nixon while consuming a cheeseburger; and Sara

Jane Moore and Lynette "Squeaky" Fromme commiserate over a bucket of Kentucky Fried Chicken, concluding with a pact to assassinate President Ford. These four characters then join the other five assassins at the end of the show to share the stage in a traditional vaudevillian chorus finale in which they reassert the idiom stated at the beginning of the show: "Everybody's Got the Right to Their Dreams." The vaudeville and the irony are thus complete when each character has had his or her individual say and then joined the rest of the dramatis personae to state their common approach in song-and-dance format. In utilizing this type of structure and other motifs of Americana, Sondheim again offers a juxtaposition of the romantic—an upbeat tour of American musical nostalgia—with the grotesque—the assassination of American presidents, and indeed of the American Dream itself.[3]

It was in this strident manner that *Assassins* asked American theatre audiences to question the fabric of the social environment that produced nine killers (or would-be killers) of presidents. Some critics dismissed the show as strictly another example of Sondheim's pessimistic approach, sharing John Lahr's evaluation of Sondheim as nothing more than a "laureate of dissolution."[4] For those harboring this opinion *Assassins* was by its nature unappealing; however, to many other American theatregoers, *Assassins* seemed inappropriate for more political reasons, since it appeared to contrast with a reigning sense of patriotism evident in the early 1990s.

During this time the prevailing mood was optimistic on the heels of economic prosperity in the 1980s, and Americans appeared ready to reflect inward and evaluate their past as they entered the final decade of the twentieth century. The country had not participated in wartime combat since its involvement in the Vietnam War, and domestic developments such as the explosion of mass communication via the Internet reinforced a reigning sense of advancement and confidence among Americans. Then in January of 1991, during previews of *Assassins* before its opening at Playwrights Horizons, the United States began formal participation in the Gulf War, its first war in almost twenty years. Reasons the presidential administration cited for American military participation centered on the United States' responsibility as a world leader to enforce international law. In response American sentiments of nationalism and patriotism soared, and the thought of critically evaluating the social structure of a leading world power in a theatrical venue became more distasteful as American military personnel fought abroad.

For most American critics *Assassins* was distasteful in the sense that it served to portray the most disgraceful events of the past during a time when Americans should have been rallying in support of their nation. Public opinion at this time decried any questioning of the country's political or social practices, viewing such questioning as blatant disrespect to those fighting the war and to those at home who expressed unwavering support for the war effort. According to Frank Rich, reviewing the production for the *New York Times* the day following its opening, "[the message explored in *Assassins*] is not a message that audiences necessarily want to hear at any time, and during the relatively jingoistic time of war in which this production happens to find itself, some may regard such sentiments as incendiary."[5] This was a period in which wartime politics dictated the role of theatre in society and when Americans appeared to focus their attention on unquestioning patriotism rather than self-reflection. As a result, any context that portrayed sardonic commentary on American political and social ideals became taboo, as had many of the themes explored in Sondheim's past musicals.

Moreover, it seems that the Gulf War exerted a type of silent influence over what might be deemed appropriate in the realm of theatrical representation during this time. With the exception of Frank Rich's remarks, most reviews of *Assassins* did not refer to inappropriate timing or a hesitance to question domestic social practice during wartime; rather they chose to avoid any acknowledgment of the piece as valid social commentary. Critics stated that the entire idea of presenting such a solemn theme as assassination in this type of ironic manner was inappropriate or even immoral. According to Jack Kroll, who reviewed the show for *Newsweek* in February of 1991, "[y]ou can swallow the savage comedy, but not the show's moral fuzziness. . . . [The phrase] 'everybody's got the right to their dreams' is a pretty pathetic rationale for the complex questions that Sondheim does raise."[6] Kroll and others were offended by the idea of portraying the assassins as rational people whose misguided actions originated as responses to frustrations shared by many Americans. Allowing these killers a forum in which to express their opinions seemed perverse and unnecessary; beyond this observation these critics did not look for any deeper meaning.

Other reviewers denied the validity of the show's premise, stating that the concept was weak since the assassins throughout American history share no common foundation. Mimi Kramer, writing for the *New Yorker* that February, adopted this view, saying that the show contained "no structure, no conceit—nothing tying together this hodgepodge of only superficially connected incidents."[7] The implication is that these nine attempts on presidents' lives are not indicative of any problem in American social practice; rather they are a series of coincidental events. According to this view any social commentary one might attempt to glean from the musical would be rendered invalid by the fact that the assassinations and attempted assassinations simply constituted a series of unrelated historical phenomena. This idea of the assassins as idiosyncrasies, rather than results of any established social structure, was reflective of a larger wartime societal atmosphere that dictated a noncritical view of American social practice.

Other critics decried Sondheim's ironic approach to such a serious topic as assassination. For example, *Time* critic William A. Henry III criticized the lighthearted style of the songs, saying that there is "an inherent contradiction between deploring the folk mythification of assassins and sustaining that very process by having a singer-narrator twang knowing ditties about the killers."[8] Henry thus expressed disapproval of Sondheim's noted technique of allowing the overall idea of the show to dictate its structure, either not understanding or choosing to ignore the intended irony associated with portraying these traditionally labeled villains in a romanticized manner. The "inherent contradiction" between content and structure that Henry observed is very much present in the work and could be said to contribute to its value as social commentary; however, Williams and others did not acknowledge such a possibility. This again reflects the unwillingness of reviewers to address in a complex manner Sondheim's stylistic choices lest they suggest a need to look deeper into social commentary than deemed appropriate given the mood of wartime patriotism. Thus, although most reviewers did not state their criticism of *Assassins* as a response to the atmosphere created by the war effort, they chose to deny the validity of any premise within the show that might have been interpreted as derisive in the fervent atmosphere of the wartime political climate. Reviews such as these, coupled with the early warnings of a slumping economy, contributed to *Assassins'* premature closing after seventy-two performances at Playwrights' Horizons and to its subsequent failure to move to Broadway in 1991.

Undeterred, however, *Assassins'* creators prepared to present the show on the London theatrical scene the following year. London critics were collectively more gracious than American critics had been, celebrating the piece as a demonstration of Sondheim's witty creative genius and reflecting overall audience identification with the show. In part this reaction can be attributed to production elements that were added for the London debut. In response to Off-Broadway reviews that proclaimed the show's inappropriateness and insensitivity, Sondheim added a song—"Something Just Broke"—to the London production. Serving as a precursor to the assassins' final number, the song allows a chorus of American citizens throughout history to share their memories of the assassinations and attempted assassinations, along with the feelings of uneasiness and loss that accompanied each example of the American Dream gone wrong:

> OTHERS: And I wondered: . . . I was scared of . . . What would follow . . .
> HOUSEWIFE: Something to be mended.
> STOCKBROKER: Made me wonder who we are . . .
> HOUSEWIFE: Something we'll have to weather—
> . . . .
> OTHERS: I'll remember it forever . . .
> HOUSEWIFE: Nothing has really ended—
> OTHERS: Where I was, What I was doing . . .
> HOUSEWIFE: Something's just been suspended.
> OTHERS: Like a flash . . .
> HOUSEWIFE: Something just broke.

With the addition of this chorus number, audience members were offered a perspective with which they could identify fully and comfortably prior to the assassins' cynical return to assert their unity in the show's conclusion. In conjunction with this adjustment to the script, the show's producers included in the playbill an article by American psychiatrist and author Robert Jay Lifton, reprinted from a 1990 edition of the *New York Times*. In it Lifton analyzed the ways in which *Assassins* in the planning stages promised to be an effective psychological analysis and tool through which audiences might directly and rationally confront the motivations that characterize the behavior of American assassins. Lifton stated that "we examine assassins in order to know ourselves as a society. . . . We confront their act, and the feelings of deadness behind it, in the service of more humane efforts toward personal and national vitality."[9] This preface offered audiences a perspective through which to contextualize and relate to the show as an analytical piece, perhaps avoiding some of the shock felt by earlier audiences as they attempted to assimilate the show's content.

Partially because of these added elements, the structure and content of the show itself were accepted in London with an openness that was not present in the American response to *Assassins*. More significant, perhaps, Great Britain has an extended tradition of sharp political and social satire, perhaps not completely accessible to American audiences. As American writer Linda Winer phrased it in 1992, "The English have a popular tradition of political theatre, and until the social discontent of the last year of two, we have had almost none."[10] From Shakespeare to Oscar Wilde to Joe Orton, British playwrights have served audiences biting satire as social and political food for thought, paralleling a similar tradition found in the literary works of George Orwell and others. Therefore, *Assassins* found success in response to a British sensibility that allowed audiences to identify with Sondheim's use of irony as a vehicle for self-reflection, regardless of its strict focus on American historical phenomena. According to one British reviewer, "the show's specific Americanness never feels alien; no background knowledge is assumed— the feelings are universal."[11] London reviewers tended to receive the assassins' behavior as a product of global dysfunction rather than as an American phenomenon, and they wrote freely of this behavior and its apparent message to audiences to evaluate the social structure in which they participate. British critics also offered theories on why the show had been received so poorly in America, citing the United States' "ultra-patriotic mood"[12] during the Gulf War, coupled with a hesitance on the part of Americans to question their own political and social behavior. Thus, in evaluating their American counterparts, British critics sensed the prevalence of patriotism over the urge to self-reflect.

Reactions such as those in Great Britain indicated the launch of a more socially objective and global perspective on *Assassins* than that which had greeted the initial production. Despite the distinctly American flavor of the show, or perhaps because of it, producers and audiences of other nationalities took notice and began to contextualize the themes explored in the show within the flavors of their own national and social environments. A successful 1994 production in Toronto, Canada, elicited positive and thoughtful responses from its critics, who wrote that the piece was disturbing yet provocative and important in terms of encouraging its audiences to evaluate their positions and behavioral choices as members of a social system. Canadian reviewer Karen Bell wrote that "Sondheim's musicals succeed, partly because of his ability to exploit his appreciation of the darker side of human existence—and this examination gives the discerning theatre-goer a satisfying theatre experience."[13] Canadian audiences, like London audiences, viewed *Assassins* as a uniquely clever embodiment of theatre as food for thought rather than as a perversion of a subject that could only be considered taboo when presented in musical theatre form.

Four years later, in 1998, the role of *Assassins* as reflective social and political commentary in a global context expanded when the show was presented in concert form at the Beit Lessin Theatre in Tel Aviv, Israel, in memory of Israeli prime minister Yitzhak Rabin's assassination three years earlier. It was apparently the first time the show appeared in response to a specific political event outside the United States; and it introduced the idea that *Assassins,* which had been labeled immoral and inappropriate in its manner of addressing the sensitive issue at hand, might be presented with the express purpose of honoring and respecting a victim of assassination. Producers in Israel felt the need to present the show "because of the enormity of Rabin's assassination, because of what has happened since and because of their and others' conviction that 'the next murder is unavoidable,' as [show director] Ashkenazi puts it."[14] The show's messages concerning social awareness and its resonance with ongoing political and social turbulence in Israel placed it in an immediate global context that allowed it to speak to the role of theatre in general, and of this piece in particular, in provoking social sensitivity among audiences. Writing for the *Jerusalem Post*, reporter Helen Kaye described the production's relevance in the context of Israeli social theatre:

> In 1990 [when the show was conceived] *Assassins* wouldn't have projected the menace it does today, when it is a grim reverberation of those shots three years ago. At the recently concluded Acre Festival, there were three plays that reflected on Rabin's murder. And the Habimah National Theatre will present *Three Years On*, whose 12 performances have already been sold out to high schools all over the country. There will probably be more.[15]

In this context *Assassins* had become what it seems Sondheim had intended—a vehicle for questioning a constantly evolving social structure that produces murderers of political figures. Unlike the London and Canadian productions, the Israeli production responded to a devastating political event unique to that country. Meanwhile, critical and audience reception in Israel reflected a different approach to the piece than that expressed in America—it was seen as a vehicle for social awareness rather than an attack on the social fabric. In the Israeli production the musical's reflection of social history acquired increased relevance as it afforded opportunities for audiences of various backgrounds to ask pertinent questions regarding their own current and past social and political struggles.

In conjunction with the increased relevance of *Assassins* to a global social and political environment, a number of smaller-scale American producers who saw the show's potential in this sense also sought to present *Assassins* following its 1991 closing Off-Broadway. Such productions, which could operate on lower budgets and were thus less risky than a full-scale Broadway production, were mounted successfully in Washington, DC, St. Louis, and Philadelphia, as well as at smaller regional theatres, progressive community theatres, and numerous college campuses throughout the United States. By 2001 *Assassins*, which had gained acclaim in a multitude of theatrical circles around the country in addition to the aforementioned international forums, also gained funding to be produced on Broadway as part of the subscription season of the Roundabout Theatre Company at the Music Box Theatre, slated for opening in November of that year. Production plans were in full swing by early September, with rehearsals set to begin later that month, when the terrorist attacks of September 11 took Americans by surprise and temporarily brought most of the nation's activity to a halt. Tourists were in no mood to travel, and entertainment, particularly musical theatre, was the last thing on the minds of New Yorkers as they mourned lost loved ones and worked to piece together the shattered backbone of their city.

In the weeks and months following the attacks, Broadway theatres struggled to stay afloat, with attendance decreasing as much as 80 percent. Several shows, such as *Kiss Me, Kate* and *The Rocky Horror Show,* were forced to close; and actors', musicians', and technicians' unions negotiated dramatic pay cuts in order to maintain even the long-running musicals such as *Rent, Les Misérables,* and *Phantom of the Opera.*[16] As with other new shows, *Assassins'* opening was immediately postponed; but the show's content introduced an additional element of complexity that caused many to question whether the production of a piece dealing with the assassination of American presidents could ever be deemed appropriate after the grievous terrorist attacks on the nation. Of particular concern was a monologue contained in the musical in which the character Sam Byck reveals his plan to crash a plane into the White House in order to assassinate President Nixon. In the wake of the air attacks of September 11, Americans were averse to such imagery in any forum.

The plane reference, coupled with the show's blatant questioning of American social and political practice, caused the production team to postpone the show's opening indefinitely. Sondheim and Weidman explained the decision in a public statement: "*Assassins* is a show which asks audiences to think critically about various aspects of the American experience. In light of Tuesday's murderous assault on our nation and on the most fundamental things in which we all believe, we, the Roundabout, and director Joe Mantello believe this is not an appropriate time to present a show which makes such a demand."[17]

Sondheim and Weidman sensed the need to monitor the national mood to determine when would be the "appropriate time" to present the show, and Sondheim did assert the possibility that *Assassins* might be presented sometime during the following year. In place of opening night the cast and production team also assembled for a single, private reading on November 12, asserting the show's momentum and the prospect of a future Broadway production following America's recovery from the recent disaster.

As remnants of the disaster were slowly repaired and Americans began to reflect on how such an event could have resulted within the prevailing global atmosphere, the questions raised in *Assassins* adopted newfound significance, not just as reflection on a domestic social level but also as reflection on America's place in the worldwide social milieu. According to some analysts of the theatre scene, the reputation *Assassins* had earned as a vehicle for thoughtful social commentary made the idea of a production even more relevant in the wake of the mass assassination of September 11. Todd Haimes, artistic director of the Roundabout Theatre Company, told the *Sondheim Review* that "We're definitely going to do it. . . . I do believe that the piece is more relevant now than it ever was. It will resonate more than ever. But I think to try to do it six weeks after September 11 would have been perverse."[18] The recovery process would prove to be long and difficult, and it would be some time before Americans would embrace a theatre presentation that dealt directly with issues of political and social destruction.

While Haimes and others were defending the piece, many writers maintained that political events continued to make *Assassins* off-limits. *Boston Herald* writer Stephen Schaefer effectively summed up these views, asserting that *Assassins* "is now totally out of sync with the country's mood. Though officially the show is 'postponed,' most believe it's permanently shelved."[19] After the very fabric of the nation had been torn by the attacks, the shock and overwhelming sense of hurt and loss that most Americans felt precluded the ability to further question American values in any way, certainly not in a way that placed those values in an ironic or humorous context.

In keeping with the national mood, this type of sensitivity characterized most critics' reactions in the months following the attack, not exclusively in reference to *Assassins* but to other forms of theatre, music, film, and visual art. Humor columns, periodicals, and television shows were canceled; action movies were placed on hold; and numerous popular songs were avoided on the airways. In the words of humorist Dave Barry, "No humor column today. I don't want to write it and you don't want to read it."[20] Through two world wars and several economic downturns, humorous entertainment had always been a distraction from adversity for Americans, but with tragedy hitting so close to home, the mood of America seemed to have undergone a permanent change.

In response to this mood in late 2001, however, some Americans saw the need for self-reflection and even humor elevated by the recent disaster. Eloquent critics began to write sensitively about the role of art, and specifically the role of theatre, in this self-reflection and in America's recovery process. In October theatre critic Robert Brustein wrote in the *New Republic* of the need to be reminded "of the obligations of art in a bad time, of why literature and drama continue to remain relevant despite our horrifying glimpses into the darkness of the human heart. . . . The American theatre currently stands, like Estragon and Vladamir, under that leafless tree in Beckett's blasted plain. The show can't go on. It must go on."[21]

Brustein argued that it is the duty of theatre artists to assert the continuing importance of asking questions and finding answers, even when the mood of the public deems otherwise. Without this constant questioning, the terrorist attacks of September 11 would be responsible not only for the deaths of their immediate victims but for the death of the nation's spirit as well. In response to these feelings, a panel of theatre artists met in November of 2001 to discuss their role in the recovery process, concluding that the work they create adopts increasingly significant meaning in a post-9/11 America. As a contributor to the panel, Broadway actor Mandy Patinkin stated, "Everything has an echo, a reverberation, that is different since the attacks. I don't think art itself will be any different, but it will be heard with greater echo."[22] Thus, theatre in the eyes of these artists gained a heightened voice in response to the attacks. Discussions and written responses such as these called theatre artists to action and called audiences to look to the work of these artists for reflection, not simply in spite of the recent tragedy but also because of it.

Other theatre artists slowly but surely responded to these calls to action. For example, Simon Watson, director of the Downtown Arts Project, regrouped his small staff to rescue his organization from obliteration and assured the public of the Arts Project's return in 2002. Spokespersons for organizations specializing in experimental and cutting-edge theatrical pieces, including the Public Theatre, Lincoln Center Festival, and Brooklyn Academy of Music, stated their intent to continue their tradition of presenting provocative works to the American public.[23]

As audiences did indeed return in greater numbers during the years that followed the attacks, plans to revive *Assassins* reemerged. Now the Broadway production, like the 1998 Israeli concert production, could be presented in response to a tragedy not specifically enumerated in the script itself but that had produced some of the same feelings of loss and confusion described by Sondheim in "Something Just Broke." Audiences could now share a fresh understanding of these feelings and come together in an attempt to understand the workings of the global society that made possible such horrific events. Librettist John Weidman observed in 2004 that "[o]n some level, people are more open to material that raises questions without giving simple answers. . . . After 9/11 we're all potential victims and in a sense potential combatants."[24] The terrorist attacks displayed firsthand the assassination of the American Dream, not by a domestic source this time but a global one; in response Americans learned to view themselves as others view them, as potential victims in a world with no easy answers. *Assassins* could no longer be dismissed—as it had been by some critics in 1991—as a study of unrelated events within American history; now, changed by the perspectives of international audiences and the firsthand American experience of terrorism, the show resonated in the aftermath of a global crisis that could not easily be discounted.

Assassins opened successfully for a limited engagement on Broadway, produced by the Roundabout Theatre Company in Studio 54 on April 22, 2004, and ran through July 18, 2004, receiving five Tony Awards. Notably, the show won the Tony Award for Best Revival of a Musical, considered in this category even though this run was in reality the show's Broadway debut. Ultimately, the show ran for more performances than planned: a total of 101. Some critics commented on the risky nature of presenting the piece while America continued to fight the war on terror abroad, but they addressed the issue as a topic of debate rather than avoiding it altogether, as critics had done during the Gulf War. In addition, reviews of the production were overall favorable and respectful of the show's provocative thematic and structural elements. *New York Times* reviewer Ben Brantley stated that the show was "misunderstood" and that "Mr. Sondheim and Mr. Weidman are simply posing a question that arises in many people's minds when they read accounts of shocking, irrational crimes: 'Why would someone do that?'"[25] Though the show closed, as did a number of others in 2004, because of low attendance attributed to a less-than-favorable economy, it was received in a public atmosphere that appeared more wary and more socially analytical than that surrounding its audiences in 1991. American audiences could no longer disregard the horrific political and social events in their midst and were more willing to confront the tough social questions raised by them.

Today, in response to shows like *Assassins,* we continue to recognize the role of theatre in questioning our social and political environments; and we place our rationalization in a globally expanding context. As London writer Mark Steyn phrased it in an article on *Assassins* less than two months after the terrorist attacks, "Anarchists were very much the international terrorists of the day."[26] The relevance of *Assassins* and of pieces like it will not diminish as long as the world remains a place where we must continue to ask questions in order to understand our changing political and social surroundings.

Notes

1. In *Pacific Overtures* (1975) greed drives characters that take on the persona of entire nations guided by the need for political power and imperialism. In *Sweeney Todd* (1979) the longing for revenge transforms the lead character into a mass murderer who slits throats Jack-the-Ripper style and deposits his victims' bodies into a grinder to be cooked and sold to a ravenous London public in the form of meat pies. In *Into the Woods* (1987) a hodgepodge of fairy-tale characters learn that the only way to conquer the threat of a giant in their midst is to work together, despite their innate selfishness, which drives such characters as Cinderella's Stepmother, who trims her daughters' feet so they might fit more easily into Cinderella's slipper. Each of these pieces and several of Sondheim's other shows challenge audiences to define their own social relationships and self-awareness in a constantly evolving modern world, a world that often seems uncannily reflected in the strange worlds of Sondheim's characters.

2. See Geoffrey Block, "Assassins," *American Music* 11, no. 4 (1993): 507–9.

3. The finale song itself also represents a piece of Americana, recalling a playful fairground rhythm that both introduces and concludes the musical. According to musical analysts James Lovensheimer and Stephen Banfield various other rhythmic, harmonic, and melodic references in *Assassins* recall traditional early and later American styles. For example, Sondheim includes the presidential march, "Hail to the Chief," woven into repeating motifs throughout the piece, as well as references to a John Phillip Sousa march ("How I Saved Roosevelt"), the cakewalk, church hymn, and parlor waltz (Guiteau's "I Am Going to the Lordy"), the barbershop quartet ("Gun Song"), and the popular love ballad (Hinckley and Fromme's "Unworthy of Your Love"). See James Lovensheimer, "Unifying the Plotless Musical: Sondheim's *Assassins*," *ISAM Newsletter* 24, no. 2 (2000); and Stephen Banfield, *Sondheim's Broadway Musicals* (Ann Arbor: University of Michigan Press, 1993), 56–59.

4. Quoted in Joanne Gordon, *Art Isn't Easy: The Achievement of Stephen Sondheim* (Carbondale: Southern Illinois University Press, 1990), 17.

5. Frank Rich, "Sondheim and Those Who Would Kill," *New York Times,* Jan. 28, 1991, late edition, C19.

6. Jack Kroll, "The Killing of Presidents," *Newsweek,* Feb. 4, 1991, 72.

7. Mimi Kramer, "Point Blank," *New Yorker,* Feb. 11, 1991, 68–69.

8. W. A. Henry III, "Glimpses of Looniness," *Time,* Feb. 4, 1991, 62.

9. Robert Jay Lifton,, "Assassination: The Ultimate Public Theater: The Assassination as American Drama," *New York Times,* Sep. 9, 1990.

10. Ibid.

11. Ian Shuttleworth, "Assassins," *City Limits,* Oct. 30, 1992, http://www.cix.co.uk/~shutters/reviews/92126.htm (accessed Sep. 21, 2005).

12. Linda Winer, "Sharing Stages, If Not Audiences," *Newsday,* Nov. 22, 1992.

13. Karen Bell, "Assassins," *Performing Arts and Entertainment in Canada* 29, no. 1 (fall 1994/winter 1995): 10–11.

14. Helen Kaye, "Looking into Murderers' Minds," *Jerusalem Post,* Oct. 28, 1998, 9.

15. Ibid.

16. See Wayne Hoffman, "World Trade Center Attacks Leave Broadway Reeling," *Billboard,* Sep. 29, 2001, 6.

17. Sarah Beaumont, "Something Just Broke: Will *Assassins* Reach Broadway Post Sept. 11?" http://www.sondheim.com/news/something_just_broke.html (accessed March 22, 2005).

18. Paul Salsini, "When Is an 'appropriate' Time for *Assassins?*" *Sondheim Review* 8, no. 3 (winter 2002), http://www.sondheimreview.com/v8n3.htm#article (accessed Sep. 21, 2005).

19. Stephen Schaefer, "Too Close to Reality: Entertainment Industry Shuffles Its Schedule in Wake of Terrorist Attacks," *Boston Herald,* Sep. 18, 2001.

20. Quoted in James Poniewozik, "What's Entertainment Now?" *Time South Pacific,* Oct. 8, 2001, 66–68.

21. Robert Brustein, "No Time for Comedy," *New Republic,* Oct. 8, 2001, 29.

22. Quoted in Rebecca M. Milzoff, "Panel Grapples with Role of Art after Sept. 11," *Harvard Crimson Online,* http://www.thecrimson.com/article.aspx?ref=123793 (accessed Sep. 21, 2005).

23. See Justin Davidson, "The Next New York," *Newsday,* April 26, 2002.

24. See Frederick M. Winship, "Sondheim's *Assassins* Is a Bull's-Eye Hit," *United Press International,* May 8, 2004, 7; and Robert Hofler, "Past and Present: Veterans of Original Productions Applaud Updates," *Variety,* May 17, 2004, B2.

25. Ben Brantley, "A Demon Gallery of Glory Hounds," *New York Times,* April 23, 2004.

26. Mark Steyn, "In the Wake," *New Criterion,* Nov. 1, 2001, 41–46.

Symposium Response

Alan Woods and Bruce A. McConachie

ALAN WOODS: Many years ago, at the old American Theatre Association convention, I was on a panel that had a respondent, a then-senior professor from one of the great state universities, who proceeded to tear each of the papers apart in the way of a graduate seminar director, pointing out the flaws and dangers of each one. I had been the last person to speak on the panel, so I sat there, thinking the equivalent of "Oh Merdre." He got to me and said that because I had failed to submit my paper in advance, he was unable to critique it, which of course made me feel very good but also very smug because I thought, "You couldn't listen to it?"

I'm not going to follow that model of response, and I do apologize to those people on the first panel on Friday that I had to miss because of the way my schedule had to work for getting here. First of all, it seems to me that this was an entirely successful symposium in many ways. I found all of the papers fascinating; I learned a huge amount of material about the various topics that were covered and from a number of perspectives, all of which I found interesting and viable and valid; you all are to be congratulated for having come through with thought-provoking papers that dealt with a variety of aspects of this year's topic. So my comments are going to be more structural than anything else. I want to comment on what I noticed about the panels and papers overall, tempered a little by this morning's panel, which skewed in a very real way where I was going with my general comments.

I was struck after Friday afternoon and yesterday that many of the research questions being asked, and the ploys and strategies being undertaken to resolve or approach those research questions, were in fact shockingly traditional. And I say that without meaning to be overly censorious or harshly negative. Almost all of the research—and this was mentioned a couple of times in various comments—was text driven; it was based on published texts and exploration of available textual material, which is a very traditional way of doing scholarship and research. It struck me that it was reinscribing a somewhat conservative kind of scholarship. I found very few—and I'm not denigrating the papers' quality by saying that, because the papers were of very high quality and were all ultimately publishable in *Theatre Symposium,* but I was startled at how few of the papers (there were a couple of exceptions)—dealt in any depth with performance and production concerns and realities. We are, for the most part, theatre people, but we seem to still be mired— and I use that word advisedly—in the traditional text-based, as opposed to performance-based, kinds of concerns. The sorts of concerns that we were in fact hearing this morning that were far more production centered and production oriented, I would have loved to have heard more about that in the space of some of the other papers and reports. And I should also have started my comments tonight with the caveat that, of course, we were hearing for the most part, quite clearly, little chunks of much larger research projects and that the twenty minutes to present in this context is always an arbitrary and forced one—and several people commented on that as they presented papers. I still do want to hear more about "How I Hate to Get Up in the Morning" from Rebecca [Rugg], and everyone essentially expressed regrets at having to leave out important elements. Again, that's another caveat that I should have expressed at the outset.

But it does seem to me that production and performance concerns are crucial to almost all the topics we were dealing with, and again, I know how hard that is. I know it's almost impossible when you are dealing—as Eva [Krivanec] was—with something that happened eighty or ninety years ago. It's very difficult to begin the process of reconstructing who those performers were. We touched on it glancingly last night when Gus [Sponberg] showed us the photograph of Henry Fonda and by implication essentially said that the production of *Mister Roberts* was informed by the weight of who Henry Fonda was and what Henry Fonda had been doing for the past fifteen years before returning to stage performance. Now again, Gus never fully articulated that, and I talked to him afterward and told him that I wished he had made that explicit because it seems to me that stands in a very large measure for explaining the attraction and appeal of *Mister Roberts.* It is a lightweight fluffy Broadway comedy, and in terms of the commodity theatre it could be nothing else, but it was given an additional weight and significance in performance by the fact of who was on the stage doing it, that it was Tom Joad playing Mister Roberts, and that gave it a weight and a significance that is not there in the text. In the performance it became a significant political-social statement about the nature of warfare that is not textually based. So the performance aspect is something I would have liked to have heard much more about. I would have liked to have heard much more of the significance that Anne Fletcher began her paper with, charmingly: the phenomenological approach. The awareness of— as Bruce McConachie has published on many years back—acknowledging the choice of topics and how that choice shapes the questions that we ask and shapes where we go to look for the evidence that will answer those questions. And again, I would have liked more self-consciousness there. Now that may be me and who I am and where I come from and what my background is. I am aware that I am speaking to some people who are a couple of generations after me and who may be much less concerned with that.

And I also would have liked, as part of that self-consciousness, a little more awareness about who is in the room, who's literally in the room here at this symposium. Who are the voices that are absent and referred to only glancingly? Several of us gave papers that dealt with, for example, racism, but I couldn't help noticing that we are generally uniform in our ethnicity, with one shining exception, and again, that's an interesting factor that should at least be acknowledged. What does that bring to bear on our topics and how do we choose? And again, the kinds of questions that we seek to ask, it seems to me, need a whole other series of self-conscious questions. I was pleased to hear Lisa [Channer] talking this morning specifically about the connections between the outside world and the performance phenomena related to *The Trojan Women* that were being discussed and described. That seems to me highly essential. Christopher [Koch] brought that in last night with his discussion of Kabuki during the American occupation.

I am not necessarily saying that the papers should have dealt more with the political or social world outside of the theatre because the twenty-minute time limit often prevented that. I live and work in an intensely political environment, which has become more politically intense within the last year. Ohio State's student paper is now running full-page ads that say "Students! Are your professors discussing inappropriate things in your classroom? Here's a website where you can go to check and see what your options are!" It doesn't ask whether your theatre professor is talking about politics, but it does state that, unless your professor is teaching political science, he or she should not be talking about President Bush and the war. There is currently a bill being

proposed before the Ohio legislature that will redefine academic freedom as discipline specific so that my academic freedom will apply only
to my discussion of theatre. I can talk about Bush's ability to read lines
from a prompter and critique him on a performance level but not critique anything else. So again, I was hoping to hear more that might
inform me about that intensely political context in which I find myself
living.

My other critique would be that—and I've railed about this at conferences for the last thirty-odd years, as long as I've been going to them,
and I do this myself and I did it Friday night in my talk on *Porgy and
Bess*. It's so easy to use quotes from the past in hindsight and to have
at least the implicit attitude of "those poor, benighted people back however many decades ago it is—if only the State Department folks in 1952
could have understood what was really going on in the world, they
wouldn't have said this about Porgy, etc." Again, I try to guard myself
against doing that, against the smug superiority of the "modern" person
looking back on the benighted people of the past. I do it all the time
because it's effective and because some of the quotes are too good not
to use. So I understand exactly what that's about, but I urge us all, and
myself as well, because I am equally guilty of it, to guard against that.
So that's my conference response. Now, I've said some things that I
don't mean to be harshly negative. I found all of the papers that I was
able to hear to be interesting, and in each case I want to see the full
study. I want to know more about Code Pink; I want kb [saine] to find
those oral histories; I want to know more about how *Assassins* was responded to in its various permutations. So there was great value in
everything I heard, and I thank you for that. So please don't take my
comments as being other than a professor used to saying to graduate
students, "Did you consider perhaps the importance of the fact that
Porgy and Bess was written by white people?"

So I will stop there and let Bruce do the brilliant summing up of the
whole conference that's the point of this session.

BRUCE MCCONACHIE: What a setup, Alan! Well, what I want to talk
about is less individual papers, I guess, than to attempt to grapple as a
historian and theorist with a general problem that a lot of us grapple
with: which is, what are the possible theatrical responses to war or at
least to the threat of war? This is, of course, a focus of a lot of your
work, and like Alan I think it was a very successful conference, and we
got a wide variety of understandings of what the options are when theatre people take a look at war. I think this is a perduring problem. Obviously we're going to have more wars in our future, and we can take

a look all the way back to Aristophanes and Euripides. So I would like to examine this problem in a global sense and bring to bear a lot of your insights in my response here, as well as throw in a few of my own. So this will be a response to most of the papers but not all of them. I'll leave aside papers that dealt with propaganda in time of peace (or relative peace), such as *Porgy and Bess,* and a few others that were not focused specifically on the problem of a theatrical or dramatic response to war.

I think probably the way to approach this is to begin with a kind of truth, a hard truth, that war is—war is mass killing, always. War is organized slaughter. War is hell. This truism has confronted humankind, of course, for a long time. But because of the nature of war—and yes it's changed, but yes it's remained the same, as we certainly know from the Greeks and Shakespeare—because of the nature of war, I think it means that theatre people don't have a lot of options when faced with this hard truth. I'll talk a little bit later about why there are so few comedies or romances about war (I don't think *Mr. Roberts* is actually about war, by the way; I think it's about tedium and authority, and the war is kept safely offstage), but if you think about those plays and theatrical events that actually attempt to confront the reality of war, comedy is not a usual option, and I'll talk about why that's so. I think we've seen from the papers at this conference that there are two general approaches that theatre people have taken to war in the past. First, there is a moral response, an ethical response. Warfare is justified on ethical grounds—and we've heard a lot about that—or warfare is damned on ethical grounds. But in either case the approach here is strongly grounded in ethics and morality. The second approach is what I would call a material response, but perhaps a bodily or a physical response would be a better term. And that's the recognition that in the face of our imminent mortality we are reduced to our puny, grotesque, and inadequate physical bodies. We realize that we can be killed, and that realization sparks a very different kind of theatrical response from the response on ethical grounds.

I think these responses tend to run in opposite directions. Strident moralism leads to heroic self-sacrifice, either for or against the war, in which we are generally encouraged to ignore what's happening to our bodies, whereas the material, physical response leads often to a temporary overturning of morality, sometimes even a rejection of morality. It leads to the carnivalesque; it leads to the grotesque—a celebration of the body but also a derisive laughter at the body. We've seen this in a good number of papers. Now these two responses tend to polar opposites—you can either go with Falstaff or you can go with Prince

Hal, but you can't find a common meeting ground here. There's just not a lot of commonality that's possible in these two positions. So, not surprisingly, these two positions lead to very different dramatic and theatrical responses. The first, the ethical response, obviously pushes theatre and drama toward didactic melodrama, toward propaganda, and occasionally toward forms of theatre that can recognize the complex ethical problems of warfare. We can talk about Euripides; we can certainly talk about Brecht in this regard. The second, the focus on mere matter and our bodies, gets us into satire, gets us into theatre of the grotesque, ironic or parodic theatre, and a whole range of carnivalesque forms, many of which have been explored at this conference. These forms often upset the usual binaries of race and gender, and I'll be talking a little bit more about the ways in which minstrelsy works, or continued to work, during the Second World War in this regard.

So this is my general perspective on the papers I've heard and also my own gloss on warfare in general and the problems that theatre people have dealing with it. First I want to examine in a bit more detail those plays or productions that rely on a strong ethical orientation, that keep that as their base, and attempt to, of course, call forth a strong ethical response from audiences. Next I'll look at theatrical pieces that invite us to at least temporarily suspend ethical concerns, ethical judgment, and focus on our performing bodies. Finally I want to discuss the difficulty of trying to find a synthesis. I've already gestured toward this with Falstaff and Prince Hal, but I think it is the particular problem that we are faced with in the wake of 9/11 and in the wake of Iraq. It may be that we have to make a rough choice here between one or the other, that some kind of synthesis is not in the cards, given who we are and how we respond to warfare.

Regarding a theatre of strong ethical orientation: we've heard from a fair number of you about demonizing the enemy, and it's pretty clear that that's one obvious way in which theatre people have responded to warfare. Yes, there is the "other"; there's the Hun; there's the Jap; there's the—you name it. And we've got a firm right to go out and kill the Son-of-a-Bitch because if we don't kill them they're going to kill us. It's an easy ethical kind of assumption, right? And we can all point to, and many of you have, hundreds of melodramas, didactic plays, or nasty, derisive comedies (although I hesitate to call them comedies; they are more like satires) that point at the enemy and demonize the "SOB." In perhaps a lighter vein, but still a propagandistic vein, we've heard from some of you about the "Good Guys," often on the home front. There are women who are protecting our boys through their work, and they deserve to be celebrated. Nonetheless this is still a response that

158 WOODS AND MCCONACHIE

hinges on a strong ethical orientation to the general "goodness" of our side in the conflict. The Stage Door Canteen gets a parade of stars who do their job for "our boys." It's the same kind of ethical orientation that, of course, is going to drive stars to want to participate and, somewhat selflessly as well, to give of their time in what they and everyone else think is a good cause, a just cause.

We've heard about a few instances of antiwar theatre that rest on ethical demands. Probably the paper that resonates most strongly in this regard is what we heard with regard to the Catonsville Nine. A production with a strong ethical orientation, there is no doubt whatsoever how the Berrigan brothers want the rest of us to feel about the Vietnam War. Ethics, of course, from their point of view, merges with religion. Now this gives the play even a stronger ethical push, doesn't it? It's not just that humanity is opposed to this war, but God is too, from their point of view. I think this shades into more complicated ethical arguments when we get to Euripides, when we get to Brecht. Interestingly, we heard two papers on *The Trojan Women:* the first an adaptation that was sent to Kosovo with a multicultural cast that colored in interesting ways the ethical implication of what the production was doing, and then a production a couple of years ago in Auburn, Alabama, that certainly demanded an ethical response and in some ways a very troubled response from many in the audience and the cast.

Finally, I would put *Mother Courage* in this category. Brecht is a moralist. His morality is anchored in Marxism, which is a moral as well as a revolutionary point of view toward history. Brecht's look toward a future utopia in which the ethical as well as the economic problems of capitalism will be solved allows him to comment on the present destructiveness of war from that point of view. It is, nonetheless, an ethical point of view, and whether we agree with it or not, Brecht certainly saw it in that way. So his utopian vision is also a strongly ethical one.

These, then, are the kinds of papers, the range of papers, that we have heard about that deal with warfare from an ethical orientation. Second, let's look at those kinds of papers about productions that suspended ethical judgment or maybe brought it in through the back door at the end, in which there may have been a sense that war is not a good thing for living beings, humans and animals, but that generally did not place the ethical problem front and center. Instead, what was front and center onstage were physical bodies. Two papers yesterday dealt with minstrelsy in the U.S. Army during the Second World War. Minstrelsy is about the carnivalesque; it is about funny noses, big feet. It is about, to some extent, laughing at others with those characteristics; but it's also about laughing at ourselves because our bodies are inadequate. Everybody is inadequate when it comes to war, and we know this; we know about the possibility of slaughter. And certainly the front-line troops watching *This Is the Army* knew that their bodies were inadequate to modern warfare. So there is something about a celebration of the possibilities and the ridiculous qualities of the body that is right for warfare. Aristophanes certainly knew this; it is a riotous part of his theatre, and we still know this, deep down. That may be partly why those southern generals wanted to bring back old-fashioned minstrelsy. There is a certain rightness about minstrelsy during a war, despite the racism—which was certainly present.

We heard about *Rip Van Winkle* on the eve of the Civil War, if you recall, and the carnivalesque celebration of Rip's drunken body, and the grotesque bodies of Henry Hudson's crew and other aspects of grotesquerie that were a part of this early performance. We heard about *Viet Rock* and the transformation of women's bodies, the possibilities of moving among a range of roles because bodies are a lot more adept than simple gender roles will ever allow for. And of course we heard about nude bodies in *Paradise Now*. Nude bodies are perhaps the final revelation, if you will, of both the possibilities and the ridiculousness of physicality in the face of warfare. I would suggest that the Living Theatre was moving toward some kind of ethical orientation. They too, had some sort of utopia in mind—*Paradise Now*, after all, is the title— but in the end the effectiveness of the performance had much less to do with a complex ethics (it's not Brechtian) than with an Artaudian celebration of Dionysian possibility. That's the thrust of this kind of theatre, certainly. Again, it's not that ethics doesn't play any role; it's that ethics is mostly kept offstage and brought in only in a general way. The kinds of pieces that I've been talking about might be understood in general as a theatre of the carnivalesque, in which the lower extremities of the body are celebrated. Everything below the belt, that's what you want to celebrate with the carnivalesque.

The theatre of the grotesque, which is related but a bit different, can get us into irony and satire in more substantial ways than the carnivalesque can. Grotesquerie invites us to look at ethical disasters, to name them but not always to resolve them in any firm way. Theatre of the grotesque often stays at the level of irony and attack without providing any clear resolution of what to do as a next step, so it can't usually forge a new ethics out of the attitude of attack that it foregrounds.

Code Pink's attack on the war certainly revels in grotesquerie. Giving pink slips to Bush and "Rummy" is a way of satirizing the nastiness of their war. Again, there is an ethics here, but it's pretty straightforward. We know what they think: it isn't the ethical argument that is primary;

it's all about ridicule. This, in many ways, takes us back to Aristophanic satire. Aristophanes does the carnivalesque and the grotesque in some wonderful ways. We have the biting irony of *Assassins,* but *Assassins* can't quite get its mind around a new ethical orientation for what's "broke" in America. It stays pretty much at the level of irony and satire. Something may be broken, but is there a new ethics that can fix it? Well, that's a much harder nut to crack; Sondheim doesn't have to go there, and I think he's right not to try.

I would say that *Streamers* is also part of the theatre of the grotesque, which is why it's so different from Brecht's *Mother Courage.* What we have with Sergeant Cokes singing "Beautiful Streamers" to Stephen Foster's melody at the end is a mourning for the grotesquerie of warfare. It's certainly an antiwar play, but again the ethics are easy. It is not asking us to really think through and take a tough ethical stand here. It's telling us, finally, that "shit happens," and it is mourning the fact that that is the case.

Can we get ethics and carnival together in the same show as a response to war? I think it's a real stretch. Perhaps the only way that this happens is through variety theatre. *This Is the Army* had the precision drilling of military bodies—if there is anything that is an embodiment of military morality, that has to be it: righteous marching. We can see it in physical bodies, but of course it's a thrill of patriotism at the same time. Yet back-to-back—maybe not quite back-to-back, but a few acts later—we have "Mandy," and we have the grotesque bodies of minstrelsy ridiculing the flesh of all of us. An interesting contrast, but you're not going to find them in the same number, for heaven's sake; they have to be separated by a few other numbers. You can't do both at the same time. You don't get military drill and "Oh Mandy, there's a minister handy," etc.

Arguably, the second wave of plays in response to 9/11 was struggling with this problem: how to deal with the mangled bodies of 9/11 and the mangled bodies in Iraq—both U.S. soldiers and Iraqi citizens. I think that may be a way in to discuss why the second wave of plays about 9/11 is not as successful as the first wave. They are trying to encompass both the reality of war, trying to keep an ethical vision, a "we" that can organize all of us into some kind of ethical orientation, but also acknowledge the pain of real bodies that cannot even accommodate the possibilities of language and identity. So we get a play such as [Jonathan] Bell's *Portraits,* which seems to me to be interestingly symptomatic of this problem. The characters are trying to get a portrait of themselves, and they are, in effect, framed onstage. It is a beautiful theatrical metaphor for an attempt at identity—we usually think of a portrait of ourselves as identifying ourselves—but these portraits are, finally, empty, as we learned in the paper. It is hard to have both a physical body and an ethical body in response to war.

It may be that a Buddhist take on this, or perhaps an ecological position, offers some possibilities for this synthesis. I was struck by [James Thompson's] paper this morning as another insight that perhaps a "theatre of beauty," based in the body, can find a synthesis that is both ethical and physical—but, boy! it's a hard stretch. Theatre of beauty seems to be a celebration of the body, but how far can that stretch ethically? I'm not really sure. Can it accommodate the possibilities that a lot of us were accommodating in our comments on World War II, the possibility of a "Just War" in which there is real pain caused to all kinds of people? We think of this as an ethical war, yet it was not a beautiful war. No war is, finally, beautiful. So I don't know if there is a meeting ground, finally, between ethics and bodies when it comes to warfare.

I want to just finish by talking about something I mentioned early on. When we think about how to reconcile ethical needs with physical needs, the usual genre that we turn to in the theatre is comedy. That's what comedy is for. That's what the wedding scene at the end of all classical comedies does. Yes, these people have physical needs, and yes there is a social ethics. How do we put them together? Well, we marry them, don't we? And there is a marriage of ethics and bodies in comedy that works—in normal times. That's how we can do it. But I think it's interesting and symptomatic that very few and perhaps none of the theatrical events we have been examining in the symposium have been about comedy. There was a mention of *Shenandoah*, which is a Civil War play, as many of you know, but what kind of Civil War play is it? It really doesn't tackle the problem of war; it tackles the problem of national reconciliation twenty-five years after war. It doesn't want to look at the horror of the Civil War; it wants to bind up our wounds and celebrate the fact that we're all in one union back together again and we better get to learn to live with it, and so we've got, you know, northerners marrying southerners. That kind of social comedy can happen fine twenty-five years later, but it isn't really a play about war; and I think we kid ourselves if we say it is.

Even Shaw's *Arms and the Man*, which is maybe the closest we get to a comedy about war, has to finish the war at the end of act 1 so we can get to the comic reconciliation at the end of act 3. Shaw knows that you can't have a comedy in the midst of war; you've got to get through with the war first. You've got to have the two former combatants worrying about how they're to get the troops back—I don't even remember the end of the play—but they're worried about the logistics of, you know, where are we going to water the horses when we have to transfer troops? So of course in the midst of this kind of mundane problem, which is postwar, it's easy enough for the two romantic leads to get together, and there can be a wedding. Shaw can't forge such a resolution at the end of *Heartbreak House,* which ends in warfare. It concludes with bombs dropping, a grotesque ending. There is no possibility for comic resolution here. So I guess I would say that our usual way of bringing bodies and ethics together, which is comedy, is not really an option for a steely, hard look at the realities of war.

Thank you.

Contributors

Kate Bredeson is a doctoral candidate at the Yale School of Drama. Last year she was a Fulbright scholar in Paris, where she conducted research for her dissertation, entitled "The End of the Absurd: Protest and Performance of May '68." She continues to live in Paris, where she writes about theatre for *GoGo,* an Anglophone cultural events publication. She is the author of the "Theatre" chapter for the recently released thirteenth edition of the *Time Out Paris* guidebook and works as a dramaturg with the New York–based company Moving Theater.

Evan Bridenstine is an assistant professor of theatre for Methodist College in Fayetteville, North Carolina. He holds an MA from Kent State University, an MFA in playwriting from the University of Virginia, and a PhD from the Ohio State University. He has published on Anne Nelson's *The Guys* in *Text and Presentation,* a journal published by the Comparative Drama conference.

Diana Calderazzo is an MA candidate and graduate teaching associate at the University of Central Florida Conservatory of Theatre. She received her BA from Smith College in 1999 and has directed professionally for the Missoula Children's Theatre in Montana and the Aracoma Story, Inc., in West Virginia. At UCF Diana was assistant director for *Picnic* and *Three Sisters,* and she completed dramaturgy work for *Assassins, Three Sisters,* and other plays. She is the winner of the 2005 Southeastern Region Kennedy Center/American College Theatre Festival Dramaturgy Award and is now preparing for national dramaturgy competition and writing her thesis, "Stephen Sondheim as Modern Wagnerian Tone Artist."

David Callaghan has published articles on the Living Theatre and 1960s performance in the *Journal of Dramatic Theory and Criticism, Works and Days, Theatre Symposium,* and *Audience Participation: Essays on Inclusion in Performance,* edited by Susan Kattwinkel (Westport, CT: Praeger, 2003). He has presented papers at various conferences, including the Southeastern Theatre Conference Theatre Symposium and the Association for Theatre in Higher Education (ATHE). The coordinator of theatre at the University of Montevallo, Alabama, he has worked professionally as a director and casting director in NYC and regionally. He holds an MFA in directing from Western Illinois University and a PhD in theatre from the CUNY Graduate Center.

Claudia Wilsch Case is a student in the Doctor of Fine Arts program in Dramaturgy and Dramatic Criticism at the Yale School of Drama and is writing her dissertation on the Theatre Guild and modern American playwriting. A recipient of the Beinecke Rare Book and Manuscript Library Dissertation Fellowship, Claudia has been a teaching fellow at Yale College and has taught theatre at Southern Connecticut State University. Her publications include translations of contemporary German plays by Theresia Walser and Kerstin Specht.

Anne Fletcher teaches courses in theatre history, dramatic literature, dramaturgy, and "styles" at Southern Illinois University, Carbondale. She has presented at regional, national, and international conferences, including the Mid-America Theatre Conference (MATC), the Southeastern Theatre Conference (SETC), the American Society of Theatre Research (ASTR), the Association for Theater in Higher Education (ATHE), and the International Federation for Theatre Research (IFTR). Her work has been published in *Theatre Journal, Theatre Symposium,* and *Theatre History Studies.* She has chapters in *A Companion to Twentieth-Century American Drama,* edited by David Krasner (Malden, MA: Blackwell, 2005); and *Experimenters, Rebels, and Disparate Voices: The Theatre of the 1920s Celebrates American Diversity,* edited by Arthur Gewirtz and James J. Kolb (Westport, CT: Praeger, 2003). Her book on Group Theatre scene designer and theorist Mordecai Gorelik is forthcoming from SIU Press.

Bruce A. McConachie is a professor of theatre and performance studies at the University of Pittsburgh. Professor McConachie received his PhD in theatre and drama from the University of Wisconsin in 1977 and is a leading scholar on American theater history and society. His scholarship includes *American Theater in the Culture of the Cold War: Producing and Contesting Containment, 1947–1962* (Iowa City: University of Iowa Press, 2003); and *Melodramatic Formations: American Theatre and Society, 1820–1870* (Iowa City: University of Iowa Press, 1992), which won the Barnard Hewitt Prize in 1993.

kb saine is an instructor of theatre at Wesleyan College, in Macon, Georgia. She earned her MFA in theatre pedagogy from Virginia Commonwealth and her BFA in English and secondary education, with minors in music and drama, from West Virginia Wesleyan College. She has returned to college-level teaching after spending two years at the George Wythe High School for the Arts, a low-income, inner-city school in Richmond, Virginia. Her professional theatre experience includes stints at Richmond Triangle Players, Theatre IV and Barkesdale Theatres, TheatreVirginia, and the Dogwood Dell, in Richmond; the Hopewell Hilltoppers in West Chester, Pennsylvania; and the Dallas Theatre Center in Dallas, Texas. Her current research projects include an intensive study of in-camp army performances during World War II, chronicling the performance history of Frances Ann Denny-Drake, and an ongoing study of the texts, performances, and sociological effects of the works of Tyler Perry.

Jim Stacy is director of theatre at Louisiana State University, Alexandria. He holds a PhD in performance studies from New York University (where he was a Shubert Fellow) and a master's degree in theatre from LSU. A native of Louisiana, he has also taught at Northern Kentucky University and Northwestern State University of Louisiana, serving at both as head of the acting program. He has published in *Theatre Journal* and the *Journal of American Drama and Theatre;* serves on the editorial board of *Southern Theatre;* and has presented at the William Inge Festival, the Southeastern Theatre Conference Theatre Symposium, and the Southwest Theatre Association (SWTA). In 1968 he campaigned for Eugene McCarthy for president.

Alan Woods is a performing arts archivist, a scholar of theatre history and literature, and a theatre practitioner as a dramaturg for professional and academic theatres. He joined the Ohio State University's Department of Theatre faculty in 1972 and has been director of the Jerome Lawrence and Robert E. Lee Theatre Research Institute since 1979. Long an advocate of accessibility, he currently administers the Eileen

Heckart Drama for Seniors Competition and teaches courses on the creation and reification of stereotypes and censorship and on the Senior Theatre movement. His most recent publications are on the career of director Julie Taymor and South African performance artist Andrew Buckland.